TIRUKKURAL OF TIRUVALLUVAR

(IN ROMAN TRANSLITERATION)

WITH ENGLISH TRANSLATION

TIRUKKURAL

OF

TIRUVALLUVAR

(IN ROMAN TRANSLITERATION)

WITH ENGLISH TRANSLATION

V. R. RAMACHANDRA DIKSHITAR

GYAN

Published by

GYAN

Gyan Publishing House
5, Ansari Road
Daryaganj, New Delhi-110002
Phone: 011-47034999, 9811692060
E-mail: books@gyanbooks.com

Distribution Network
gyanbooks.com
India, USA, Canada, UK, Australia

ISBN: 978-93-6780-507-7 (HB)

First Published, 1949

2nd Impression 2024

Printed at: Gyan Press, Delhi.

TIRUKKURAL OF TIRUVALLUVAR
(IN ROMAN TRANSLITERATION)
WITH ENGLISH TRANSLATION

Translator: V. R. RAMACHANDRA DIKSHITAR

TIRUKKUṞAḶ OF TIRUVAḶḶUVAR

(IN ROMAN TRANSLITERATION)

WITH ENGLISH TRANSLATION

TIRUKKUṚAḶ

OF

TIRUVAḶḶUVAR

(IN ROMAN TRANSLITERATION)

WITH ENGLISH TRANSLATION

BY

V. R. RAMACHANDRA DIKSHITAR, M.A.,

Professor of Indian History and Archaeology,
University of Madras

THE ADYAR LIBRARY

1949

PREFACE

MORE than four years ago Sir A. Ramaswami Mudaliar, now Dewan of Mysore, suggested that I might undertake a translation of the *Tirukkuṟaḷ* as also its transliteration. The present book is the outcome of his suggestion. To serve the needs of a wider public, it is now published in two volumes, one containing the text in Roman transliteration and the other in Tamil script, and both containing English translation. The *Tirukkuṟaḷ* of Tiruvaḷḷuvar is the pride of South India. What the *Bhagavad Gītā* is to the Sanskritist, the *Tirukkuṟaḷ* is to the lover of Tamil. In this book Tiruvaḷḷuvar treats of Muppāl, or Trivarga (*Dharma*, *Artha*, and *Kāma*). He has divided his book into three parts, the first dealing with *Aram*, the second with *Poruḷ*, and the last with *Kāma*. This Tamil classic deals *in extenso* with the moral values of life which foster neighbourliness and love among all men and women to whatever race or community they may belong. It is now nearly twenty years since I published my *Studies in Tamil Literature and History*, where I have assigned the first or second century B. C. as the date of its composition. I find no reason to change that view.

In this endeavour I have largely followed the text and consulted the translation of the *Tirukkuṛaḷ* published by Sri A. Ranganatha Mudaliar, Triplicane. Mr. R. S. Desikan of the Presidency College and the Rev. W. B. Harris of the Methodist Mission looked into the manuscript of the work and offered me valuable suggestions for which my thanks are due to them. I must also acknowledge the immense help I received from Dr. M. Varadarajan, Senior Lecturer in Tamil, University of Madras, in going through the proofs. I am indebted to the authorities of the Adyar Library, Adyar especially to Captain G. Srinivasa Murti for undertaking this publication and to Dr. C. Kunhan Raja for his co-operation. I further record my thanks to the Syndicate of the Madras University for permitting me to bring out this publication.

Madras, V. R. R. DIKSHITAR
6th May, 1949

CONTENTS

PORUṬPĀL

NOTE ON TRANSLITERATION AND DIACRITICAL MARKS

Generally the phonetical method is followed in transliteration

Long vowels are indicated thus:			ā,	ē,	ī,	ō,	ū.
c represents	....	....	च,	s'	श,	ṣ	ष.
ḍ ”	....	....	ड	ṭ	ट		
ḷ ”	....	....	ள்				
ḻ ”	....	....	ழ்				
ṇ ”	...	....	ண்				
ṉ ”	....	....	ன்				
ñ ”	....	....	ஞ்				
h ”	....	....	ஃ				
ṟ ”	....	....	ற்				

TIRUKKUṞAḶ

AṞATTUPPĀL

I. PĀYIRAM

CHAPTER 1—KAḌAVUḶ VĀḺTTU

1. Akara mudala eḻuttellām ādi
bhagavan mudaṟṟē ulaku.

2. Kaṟṟadanā lāya payanenkol vālaṟivan
naṟṟāḷ toḷā arenin.

3. Malarmis'ai ēkinān mānaḍi s'erndār
nilamis'ai nīduvāḷ vār.

4. Vēṇḍudal vēṇḍāmai ilānaḍi s'ērndārkku
yāṇḍum iḍumbai ila.

5. Iruḷs'ēr iruvinaiyum s'ērā iṟaivan
poruḷs'ēr pukaḻpurindār māṭṭu.

6. Poṟivāyiḷ ainduavittān poytīr oḻukka
neṟininṟār nīḍuvāḷ vār.

7. Tanakkuvamai illādān tāḷs'ērndārkku allāl
manakkavalai māṟṟal aridu.

8. Aṟavāḻi antaṇan tāḷs'ērndārkku allāl
piṟavāḻi nīndal aridu.

9. Kōḻil poṟiyil guṇamilavē eṇguṇattān
tāḷai vaṇaṅkāt talai.

10. Piṟavip perumkaḍal nīnduvar nīntār
iṟaivan aḍis'ērā tār.

I. PREFACE

CHAPTER 1—IN PRAISE OF GOD

1. All the letters have the letter 'A' as their origin: this world has God as its origin.

2. Of what avail is learning, if the learned do not adore the good feet of Him who is Immaculate Wisdom?

3. Those who find refuge in the great feet (of Him) who lives in the lotus of the heart (of the devotee) live eternally in heaven.

4. Those who have attained the feet of Him who has no likes or dislikes will be rid of all troubles.

5. Actions, both good and bad that spring from darkness of the mind will never touch those who ever chant the glories of the Lord.

6. Those who still the five senses and walk in truth and right will ever live.

7. Only those who have sought refuge in the feet of the peerless can shake off anxiety. Others cannot.

8. Only those who have clung to the feet of the Lord who is the sea of righteousness, will be able to sail the other seas. Others cannot.

9. The head that does not bow down before and worship the feet of the Lord of the eight attributes, will be as like the palsied senses.

10. Those who gain the feet of the Lord cross the great ocean of births: others cannot.

CHAPTER 2—VĀṈ S'IṞAPPU

11. Vāṉiṉ ṟulakam vaḻanki varudalāl
tāṉamilda meṉṟuṇaraṟ pāṟṟu.

12. Tuppārkkut tuppāya tuppākkit tuppārkkut
tuppāya tū malai.

13. Viṇṇiṉṟu poyppiṉ virinīr viyaṉulakattu
uṇṇiṉṟu uḍaṟṟum pas'i.

14. ērin uḻār uḻavar puyaleṉṉum
vāri vaḷaṃkuṉṟik kāl.

15. Keḍuppadūm keṭṭārkkuc cārvāymaṟ ṟāngē
eḍuppadūm ellām maḻai.

16. Vis'umbiṟ ṟuḷivīḻiṉ allāṉmaṟ ṟāngē
pas'umpuṟ ṟalaikāṇ paridu.

17. Neḍumkaḍalum taṉṉīrmai kuṉṟum taṭindeḻili
tāṉnalkā tāki viḍiṉ.

18. S'iṟappoḍu pūs'aṉai s'ellātu vāṉam
vaṟakkumēl vānōrkkum īṇḍu.

19. Tāṉam tavam iraṇḍum tangā viyaṉulakam
vāṉam vaḻangā teṉiṉ.

20. Nīriṉṟu amaiyādu ulakeṉiṉ yāryārkkum
vāṉiṉṟu amaiyā toḻukku.

CHAPTER 2—IN PRAISE OF RAIN

11. The world for its existence depends on unfailing rainfall: the rain may well be regarded as the nectar of life.

12. The rain is the source of all articles of food that man needs. It becomes his drink too.

13. Hunger would stalk abroad and torment this wide sea-girt world were the rains to fail in time.

14. The cultivators would cease to plough were the clouds' free supply of water to fail.

15. It is the rain that afflicts man and it is its fall that relieves him.

16. If the clouds were to withhold rain not even a blade of grass would rustle on earth.

17. Even the illimitable deep shrinks if the clouds do not pour and replenish it.

18. If the rains were to fail there would be no more offerings and festivals to the gods.

19. If the rains were to fail, there would neither be alms nor penance on this wide earth.

20. The world cannot exist without water; there will be no ceaseless supply without rainfall.

CHAPTER 3—NĪTTĀR PERUMAI

21. Oḻukkattu nīttār perumai viḻuppattu
vēṇḍum paṉuvaṟ ṟuṇivu.

22. Tuṟandār perumai tuṇaikkūriṉ vaiyattu
Iṟandārai eṇṇikkoṇ ṭaṟṟu.

23. Irumai vakaiterindu īṇḍaṟam pūṇḍār
perumai piṟangiṟṟu ulaku.

24. Uraṉeṉṉum toṭṭiyāṉ ōraindum kāppāṉ
varaṉeṉṉum vaippukkōr vittu.

25. Aindavittāṉ āṟṟal akalvis'umpu lārkōmāṉ
Indiraṉē s'ālum kari.

26. S'eyaṟkariya s'eyvār periyar s'iṟiyar
s'eyaṟkariya s'eykalā dār.

27. S'uvaioḷi ūṟōs'ai nāṟṟameṉ ṟaindiṉ
vakaiterivāṉ kaṭṭē ulaku.

28. Niṟaimoḻi māndar perumai nilattu
maṟaimoḻi kāṭṭi viḍum.

29. Guṇameṉṉum kuṉṟēṟi niṉṟār vekuḷi
kaṇamēyum kāttal aridu.

30. Antaṇar eṉpōr aṟavōrmaṟ ṟevvuyirkkum
s'entaṇmai pūṇḍoḻuka lāṉ.

CHAP. 3—ON THE GREATNESS OF RENUNCIATION

21. The one supreme thing all scriptures affirm is the great renunciation of those who walk in right conduct.

22. To measure the greatness of one who has *renounced is like reckoning the number of the dead in* this world.

23. The greatest thing on earth is the renunciation of those who understand birth and liberation.

24. He who with firmness bridles the five senses is (himself) the seed of the eternal bliss. Verily he is the seed of the immortals who with firmness bridles the five senses.

25. Indra, the Lord of the skies is himself a witness, to the might of those who have conquered their five senses.

26. The great achieve the impossible: the little cannot.

27. The world falls at the feet of one who has realised the true nature of the taste, sight, touch, sound and smell.

28. The greatness of the sages in this world is borne out by their prophetic utterances.

29. It is impossible to resist even for a minute the wrath of those who stand on the hill of virtue's actions.

30. They are the Brahmans who are righteous and love all creation.

CHAPTER 4—AṞAṈ VALIYUṞUTTAL

31. S'iṛappīṉum s'elvamum ēṉum aṛattiṉūmku
ākkam evaṉō uyirkku.

32. Aṛattiṉūmku ākkamum illai: ataṉai
maṛattaliṉūmku illai kēḍu.

33. Ollum Vakaiyāṉ aṛaviṉai ōvātē
s'ellumvāy ellām s'eyal.

34. Maṉattukkaṇ mās'ilaṉ āṭal aṉaittaṛaṉ:
ākula nīra piṛa.

35. *Aḻukkāṟu avā vekuḷi iṉṉāccol nāṉkum*
iḻukkā iyaṉṛatu aṛam.

36. Aṉṛaṛivām eṉṉātu aṛam s'eyka: maṛṛatu
poṉṛunkāl poṉṛāt tuṇai.

37. Aṛattāṛu iduveṉa vēṇḍā s'ivikai
poṛuttāṉōḍu ūrndāṉ iḍai.

38. Vīḻnāḷ paḍāmai naṉṛāṛṛiṉ ahtoruvaṉ
vāḻnāḷ vaḻi yaḍaikkun kal.

39. Aṛattāṉ varuvatē iṉbam: maṛ ṛellāṛ
puṛatta pukaḻum ila.

40. S'eyaṛpāla tōrum araṉē: oruvaṛku.
uyaṛpāla tōrum paḻi.

CHAPTER 4—ON DHARMA

31. Is there anything higher in life than Dharma? It secures glory and wealth.

32. Nothing is higher than Dharma: to forget it is wrought with greatest evil.

33. Avail yourself of all opportunities. Do not cease from practising Dharma on all possible occasions to the best of your ability.

34. Be pure in mind. That is Dharma. All else is but pompous show.

35. That course of conduct that steers clear of every desire, wrath, and offensive speech—is alone Dharma.

36. Do not postpone doing Dharma. Do it now. For it will be a never failing friend at your death.

37. Why search for the fruits of Dharma? Behold the one in the palanquin and the palanquin-bearer.

38. If one were to practise righteousness every day it would be the stone that blocks the way to re-birth.

39. Happiness springs only from Dharma. All else is sorrow and merits no praise.

40. To do good and to avoid evil must be the law of our being.

II. ILLAṞAVIYAL

CHAPTER 5—ILVĀḺKKAI

41. Ilvāḻvāṉ eṉbāṉ iyalpuḍaiya mūvarkku
nallāṟṟiṉ niṉṟa tuṇai.

42. Tuṟantārkkum tuvvā tavarkkum iṟantārkkum
ilvāḻvāṉ enbāṉ tuṇai.

43. Teṉpulattār teyvam virunduokkal tāṉeṉṟānku
aimpulattāṟu ōmbal talai.

44. Paḻiyañcip pāttūṇ uḍaittāyiṉ vāḻkkai
vaḻiyeñcal eñjñānṟum il.

45. Aṉpum aṟaṉum uḍaittāyiṉ ilvāḻkkai
paṇpum payaṉum atu.

46. Aṟattāṟṟiṉ ilvāḻkkai yāṟṟiṉ puṟattāṟṟiṉ
pōyyp peruvatu evaṉ.

47. Iyalbiṉāṉ ilvāḻkkai vāḻpavaṉ eṉbāṉ
muyalvāruḷ ellām talai.

48. Āṟṟiṉoḻukki aṟaṉ iḻukkā ilvāḻkkai
nōṟpāriṉ nōṉmai uḍaittu.

49. Aṟaṉeṉap paṭṭade ilvāḻkkai : ahtum
piṟaṉpaḻippatu illāyiṉ naṉṟu.

50. Vaiyattuḷ vāḻvānku vāḻpavaṉ vānuṟaiyum
teyvattuḷ vaikkap paṭum.

II. ON DOMESTIC VIRTUE

CHAPTER 5—ON FAMILY LIFE

41. The householder is the prop of the three orders of life in the conduct of their virtue.

42. The householder is the mainstay of the ascetics, the needy and the dead.

43. It is the supreme virtue (of the householder) to fulfil his obligations to forefathers, gods, guests, relatives and himself.

44. If one were to live in fear of infamy and partake of the remains of food (offered) one's line would never perish.

45. The life of householder marked by love and rectitude is itself virtue and its fruit.

46. Is there any gain greater in resorting to other orders of life than by pursuing the right path of the householder?

47. The life of the householder is far greater than that of one in the path of renunciation.

48. The householder who keeps others in the right path and himself does not deviate from his, does greater penance than the anchorite.

49. What is Dharma but the life of the householder? There is no greater life if it is free from reproach.

50. He who lives the true life of the householder on earth becomes one among the gods in Heaven.

CHAPTER 6—VĀḺKKAITTUṆAI NALAM

51. Maṉaittakka māṇpuḍaiya ḷākittaṟ koṇḍāṉ
vaḷattakkāḷ vāḻkkait tuṇai.

52. Maṉaimāṭci illāḷkaṇ illāyiṉ vāḻkkai
eṉaimāṭcit tāyiṉum il.

53. Illateṉ illavaḷ māṇpāṉāl : uḷḷateṉ
illavaḷ māṇāk kaḍai.

54. Peṇṇiṉ perumtakka yāvuḷa kaṟpeṉṉum
tiṇmaiyuṇ ṭākap peṟiṉ.

55. *Teyvam toḻāḷ koḻunaṟ ṟoḻuteḻuvāḷ*
peyyeṉap peyyum maḻai.

56. Taṟkāttut taṟkoṇḍāṟ pēṇit takaiśāṉṟa
śorkāttuc cōrvilāḷ peṇ.

57. Śiṟaikākkum kāppevaṉ śeyyum makaḷir
niṟaikākkum kāppe talai.

58. Peṟṟāṟ peṟiṉpeṟuvar peṇḍir perumśiṟappup
puttēḷir vāḻum ulaku.

59. Pukaḻpurin tillilōrk killai ikaḻvārmuṉ
ēṟupōl pīḍu naṭai.

60. Mangalam eṉba maṉaimāṭci : maṟṟataṉ
naṉkalam naṉmakkaṭ pēṟu.

CHAPTER 6—ON WIVES

51. She is the true partner in life who possesses all the wifely virtues and spends according to the income of her husband.

52. Home life shorn of its grace will be barren however pompous it may be.

53. If the wife abounds in virtues is there anything lacking in home? Lacking which, it lacks everything.

54. Is there anything greater than a woman if only she is the citadel of chastity?

55. Waking up she worships no other god than her husband. Verily at her very bidding it rains.

56. She is the woman who shields herself, serves her wedded lord, maintains her glory and never ceases from her toil.

57. Of what use is one's watch and ward? Her chastity is her only shield.

58. A dutiful wife inherits heaven with all its glory.

59. A cuckold knows not the lovely gait of a lion before his detractors.

60. The grace of a home is her virtue. Her blessed children are its adornment.

CHAPTER 7—PUTALVARAIP PEṞUTAL

61. Peṟumavaṟṟuḷ yāmaṟiva tillai aṟivaṟinda
makkaṭpēṟu alla piṟa.

62. Eḻupiṟappum tīyavai tīṇḍā paḻipiṟangāp
paṇpuḍai makkaṭ peṟiṉ.

63. Tamporuḷ eṉba tammakkaḷ: avarporuḷ
tamtam viṉaiyāṉ varum.

64. Amiḻtiṉum āṟṟa iṉitē: tammakkaḷ
s'irukai aḷāviya kūḻ.

65. Makkaḷmey tīṇḍal uḍaṟkiṉbam: maṟṟavar
s'oṟkēṭṭal iṉbam s'evikku.

66. Kuḻaliṉitu yāḻiṉitu eṉbatam makkaḷ
maḻalaiccoṟ kēḷā tavar.

67. Tandai makaṟkāṟṟu naṉṟi avaiyattu
mundi iruppac ceyal.

68. Tammiṟṟam makkaḷ aṟivuḍaimai mānilattu
maṉṉuyirkku ellām iṉitu.

69. Ēṉṟa poḻutiṉ perituvakkum taṉmakaṉaic
cāṉṟōṉ eṉakkeṭṭa tāy.

70. Makaṉtandaik kāṟṟum udavi ivaṉtandai
eṉṉōṟṟāṉ koleṉum s'ol.

CHAPTER 7—ON SONS

61. We do not know of any other asset than that of intelligent off-spring.

62. All the seven births no evil befalls one who is blest with good and unstained children.

63. A man's riches are his children; their riches are the fruit of their actions.

64. Sweeter than ambrosia is the food handled by the tender hand of one's children.

65. The delight of the body is the touch of one's children. The delight of the ear is their lisp.

66. The 'lute is sweet', 'the Veena is sweet', they say who have not heard the lisp of their little ones.

67. The good a father can do his son is to make him occupy the first rank in an assembly.

68. Wisdom of the child is not merely the father's delight but the delight of the world.

69. A mother's joy to hear of her son's greatness transcends that at his birth.

70. The service a son can do his father is to make the public exclaim 'see, the fruit of his father's good deeds.'

CHAPTER 8—AṈBUḌAIMAI

71. Anbiṟkum uṇḍō aṭaikkumtāḻ ārvalar
puṉkaṇṇīr pūs'al tarum.

72. Aṉbilār ellām tamakkuriyar: aṉbuḍaiyār
eṉbum uriyar piṟarku.

73. Aṉbōḍu iyainda vaḻakkeṉba āruyirkku
eṉbōḍu iyainda toḍarpu.

74. Aṉbīṉum ārvam uḍaimai aduvīṉum
naṉbeṉṉum nāṭās' s'iṟappu.

75. Aṉbuṟ ṟamarnda vaḻakkeṉba vaiyakattu
iṉbuṟṟār yaitum s'iṟappu.

76. Aṟattiṟkē aṉbus'ārpu eṉba: aṟiyār
maṟattiṟkum ahtē tuṇai.

77. Eṉbi lataṉai veyılpōlak kāyumē
aṉbi lataṉai aṟam.

78. Aṉbakat tillā uyirvāḻkkai vaṉpāṟkaṇ
vaṟṟal marandaḻirt taṟṟu.

79. Puṟattuṟuppu ellām evaṉs'eyyum yākkai
akattuṟuppu aṉbil avarkku.

80. Aṉbiṉ vaḻiyatu uyirnilai: ahtilārkku
eṉbutōl pōrtta uḍambu.

CHAPTER 8—LOVING-KINDNESS

71. Is there a bolt to fasten one's love? The trickling tears at the distress of one's friends will proclaim the love within.

72. The loveless are full of themselves but the loving lay down their lives for others.

73. They say the endless incarnation of one's spirit is for the fulfilment of love.

74. Out of love springs kindness. It in turn grows into inestimable prize of friendship.

75. The joy of heaven is but the fruit of righteous life rooted in love.

76. The ignorant say that kindness is an ally of virtue. No, it is a defence against evil too.

77. The sun dries up a boneless body. Likewise the god of righteousness destroys the loveless one.

78. To live a life void of love is like a withered tree bursting into leaf in a barren land.

79. What profits one's outward feature if one's heart is devoid of love?

80. That body where love dwells is the seat of life; all others are but skin-clad bones.

CHAPTER 9—VIRUNTŌMBAL

81. Iruntōmbi ilvāḻva tellām viruntōmbi
vēḷāṇmai s'eytaṟ poruṭṭu.

82. Virundu puṟattatāt tānuṇḍal s'āvā
maruntepinum vēṇḍaṟpāṟ ṟaṉṟu.

83. Varuvirundu vaikalum ōmbuvāṉ vāḻkkai
paruvandu pāḻpaṭudal iṉṟu.

84. Akaṉamarndu s'eyyāḷ uṟaiyum mukaṉamarndu
nalvirundu ōmbuvāṉ il.

85. Vittum iḍalvēṇḍum kollō? viruntōmbi
miccil mis'aivāṉ pulam.

86. S'elvirun tōmbi varuvirundu pārttiruppāṉ
nalvirundu vāṉat tavarkku.

87. Iṉaittuṇaittu eṉbatoṉṟu illai viruntiṉ
tuṇaittuṇai vēḷvip payaṉ.

88. Parintōmbip paṟṟaṟṟēm eṉbar viruntōmbi
vēḷvi talaippaṭā dār.

89. Uḍaimaiyuḷ iṉmai viruntōmbal: ōmbā
maḍamai maḍavārkaṇ uṇḍu.

90. Mōppak kuḻaiyum aṉiccam: mukantirindu
nōkkak kuḻaiyum virundu.

CHAPTER 9—ON HOSPITALITY

81. To keep house and to acquire wealth is only to minister to guests.

82. With a guest waiting it would not be proper to eat, even though it were nectar.

83. A life of one who daily looks after the incoming guests will never suffer from poverty.

84. Fortune smiles on the house of one who entertains with cheerful face worthy guests.

85. Does the field of one who partakes of what remains after entertaining the guest, need to be sown with seeds ?

86. He who cherishes the guests who come to him, and looks forward to new guests, will himself be the honoured guest of the gods.

87. The effects of hospitality cannot be exactly measured. They are proportionate to the worth of the guest.

88. Those who have failed in their duties to guests will regret the folly of mere hoarding.

89. To be poor amidst plenty is to despise hospitality. Such folly is only of the ignorant.

90. The *aniccam* flower withers when smelt, and the guest under a displeased look.

CHAPTER 10—INIYAVAI KŪṞAL

91. Inˢolāl ēram aḻaiyip paḍiṟilavām
s'emporuḷ kaṇḍār vāyccol.

92. Akaṉ amarntu ētaliṉ naṉṟē mukanamarndu
Inˢolaṉ ākappeṟiṉ.

93. Mukattāṉ amarndiṉitu nōkki akattāṉām
iṉs'o liṉitē aṟam.

94. Tuṉbuṟūm tuvvāmai illākum yārmāṭṭum
Iṉbuṟūm iṉs'ol avarkku.

95. Paṇivuḍaiyaṉ iṉs'olaṉ ātal oruvaṟku
aṇi : alla maṟṟup piṟa.

96. Allavai tēya aṟamperukum nallavai
nāḍi iṉiya s'oliṉ.

97. Nayaṉēṉṟu naṉṟi payakkum payaṉēṉṟu
paṇpiṉ talaippiriyāc col.

98. S'iṟumaiyuḷ nīngiya iṉs'ol maṟumaiyum
immaiyum iṉban tarum.

99. Inˢol iṉitīṉṟal kāṇpāṉ evaṉkolō
vaṉs'ol vaḻangu vatu.

100. Iṉiya uḷvāka iṉṉāta kūṟal
kaṉiyiruppak kāykavarn daṟṟu

CHAPTER 10—ON SWEET WORDS

91. Sweet are the words that fall from the lips of those who are full of guileless love and truth.

92. To speak with a pleasant look is better than to give with a cheerful heart.

93. To welcome one with a pleasant look and loving words is righteousness.

94. The torment of poverty does not befall those who have a good word to say to all.

95. Humility and loving words are only true ornaments. Others are not.

96. Vice wears out and virtue grows in one who speaks kind and wholesome words.

97. Sweetly uttered words that do good to others will light up the path of virtue.

98. Sweet and inoffensive words yield one happiness both here and hereafter.

99. Why should a man use harsh words, knowing the pleasure that sweet speech kindles?

100. Indulging in offensive words and avoiding sweet ones is like prefering the raw to a ripe fruit.

CHAPTER 11—S'EYNNAṈṞI YAṞIDAL

101. S'eyyāmaṟ s'eyda udavikku vaiyakamum vāṉakamum āṟṟral aritu.

102. Kālattiṉāl s'eyda naṉṟi s'irideṉiṉum Jñālattiṉ māṇap peridu.

103. Payaṉtūkkār s'eyda udavi nayaṉtūkkiṉ naṉmai kaḍalil peridu.

104. Tiṉaittuṇai naṉri s'eyiṉum paṉaittuṉaiyāk koḷvar payaṉterı vār.

105. Udavi varaittaṉṟu udavi udavi s'eyappaṭṭār s'ālbiṉ varaittu.

106. Maṟavaṟka mās'aṟṟār kēṇmai : tuṟavaṟka tuṉbattuḷ tuppāyār naṭpu.

107. Eḷumai eḻupiṟappum uḷḷuvar tangaṇ viḻumam tuḍaittavar naṭpu.

108. Naṉṟi maṟappadu naṉṟaṉṟu : naṉṟallatu aṉṟe maṟappadu naṉṟu.

109. Koṉṟaṉṉa iṉṉā s'eyiṉum avars'eyda oṉṟunaṉṟu uḷḷak keḍum.

110. Ennaṉṟi koṉṟārkkum uyvuṇḍām : uyvillai' s'eynnaṉṟi koṉṟa makaṟku.

CHAPTER 11—ON GRATITUDE

101. For the help rendered expecting no return even earth and heaven will prove no recompense.

102. A help timely, though small, transcends the world.

103. Help done expecting no return, if weighed will be vaster than the sea.

104. Small as millet is the help given, the wise hold it as big as a palmyra fruit.

105. Help rendered is not in terms of the return but its value depends on the receiver.

106. Forget not the companionship of the pure of heart. Give up not the friendship of those who have stood by you in hour of sorrow.

107. The good remember with gratitude, all through seven births, the friendship of those who have wiped out their suffering.

108. It is not good to forget the benefit received: but it is good to forget then and there the injury done by another.

109. The remembrance of one good act done removes from our mind the sting of a deadly injury.

110. There is salvation to those guilty of any other sin: but there is no redemption for the sin of ingratitude.

CHAPTER 12—NAḌUVU NILAIMAI

111. Takuti eṉavoṉṟu naṉṟē pakutiyāl
pāṟpaṭ ṭoḻukap peṟiṉ.

112. S'eppam uḍaiyavaṉ ākkam s'idaiviṉṟi
eccattiṟku ēmāppuḍaittu.

113. Naṉṟē tariṉum naḍuvikandām ākkattai
aṉṟē oḻiya viḍal.

114. Takkār takavilar eṉbadu avar avar
eccattāl kāṇap paḍum.

115. Kēḍum perukkamum illalla neñcattuk
kōḍāmai s'āṉṟōrkku aṇi.

116. Keḍuval yāṉeṉba taṟika: taṉneñcam
naḍuvori alla s'eyin.

117. Keḍuvāka vaiyādu ulakam naḍuvāka
naṉṟikkaṉ tankiyāṉ tāḻvu.

118. S'amaṉ s'eydu s'īrtūkkum kōlpōl amaintorupāl
Kōḍāmai s'āṉṟōrkku aṇi.

119. S'oṟkōṭṭam illadu s'eppam: orutalaiyā
uḍkōṭṭam iṉmai peṟiṉ.

120. Vāṇikam s'eyvārkku vāṇikam pēṇip
piṟavum tamapōṟ s'eyiṉ.

CHAPTER 12—ON EQUITY

111. An equity which knows no partiality is in itself a unique virtue.

112. The wealth of the upright dwindles not and passes on to their posterity.

113. Give up ill-gotten wealth though it brings in its train prosperity.

114. The just and the unjust are known by the progeny.

115. To hold the scales even unmindful of prosperity or adversity is the ornament of the wise.

116. Even an iniquitous thought spells one's ruin.

117. The world despises not the poverty of the just.

118. Not to tilt like the well poised balance is the grace of the wise.

119. Equity is the impartial expression of an unbiased mind.

120. To deal with others' goods as their own is the only true trade among traders.

CHAPTER 13—AṬAKKA MUḌAIMAI

121. Aṭakkam amararuḷ uykkum : aṭankāmai
ārirul uyttu viḍum.

122. Kākka poruḷā vaṭakkattai yākkam
adaṉinūg killai uyirkku.

123. S'eṟivaṟindu s'īrmai payakkum aṟivaṟindu
āṟṟiṉ aṭangap peṟiṉ.

124. Nilaiyiṟ ṟiriyādu aṭangiyāṉ tōṟṟam
malaiyiṉum māṇap peridu.

125. Ellārkkum naṉṟām paṇital : avaruḷḷum
s'elvarkkē s'elvam takaittu.

126. Orumaiyuḷ āmaipōl aindaṭṭakkal āṟṟiṉ
eḻumaiyum ēmāppu ḍaittu.

127. Yākāvā rāyiṉum nākākka : kāvākkāl
s'ōkāppar s'olliḻukkup paṭṭu.

128. Oṉṟāṉum tīccoṟ poruṭpaya ṉuṇḍāyiṉ
naṉṟu ākātāki viḍum.

129. Tīyiṉāl s'uṭṭapuṇ uḷḷāṟum : āṟādē
nāviṉāl s'uṭṭa vaṭu.

130. Kadangāttuk kaṟṟaṭangal āṟṟuvāṉ s'evvi
aṟampārkkum āṟṟiṉ nuḻaindu.

CHAPTER 13—ON SELF-CONTROL

121. Self-control places one among the gods; lack of it leads one to the darkness of hell.

122. There is no greater wealth than self-control; treasure it as your wealth.

123. If one knows the value of self-control and restrains oneself it will bring one fame.

124. Loftier than a mountain is the greatness of one who practises self-control.

125. Humility becomes all; but it crowns anew the wealthy.

126. If one were to withdraw within oneself the five senses like a tortoise, it would afford him protection all the seven births.

127. Whatever else you may not control, control your tongue, lest you should repent your indiscreet words.

128. One would lose the fruits of one's good actions, if one word of evil were to land another in trouble.

129. The blister caused by fire will heal. But the brand of a bitter tongue will never heal.

130. The God of righteousness seeks one who is on guard against anger and attains self-control through knowledge.

CHAPTER 14—OḺUKKAMUḌAIMAI

131. Oḻukkam viḻuppam taralāṉ oḻukkam
uyiriṉum ōmbap paḍum.

132. Parintōmbik kākka oḻukkam : terintōmbit
tēriṉum ahtē tuṇai.

133. Oḻukka muḍaimai kuṭimai : Iḻukkam
iḻinda piṛappāy viḍum.

134. Maṛappiṉum ōttuk koḷalākum pārppāṉ
piṛappoḻukkam kuṉṛak keḍum.

135. Aṛukkā ṛuḍaiyāṉkaṇ ākkam pōṉṛillai
oḻukkam ilāṉkaṇ uyarvu.

136. Oḻukkattiṉ olkār uravōr iḻukkattiṉ
ētam paḍupākku aṛindu.

137. Oḻukkattiṉ eytuvar mēṉmai : iḻukkattiṉ
eytuvar eytāp paḻi.

138. Naṉṛikku vittākum naloḻukkam : tīyoḻukkam
eṉṛum iḍumbai tarum.

139. Oḻukka muḍaiyavarku ollāvē tīya
vaḻukkiyum vāyāṛ s'olal.

140. Ulakattōḍu oṭṭa oḻukal palakaṟṟum
kallār aṛivilā tār.

CHAPTER 14—ON RIGHT CONDUCT

131. Right conduct exalts one. So it should be prized above one's life.

132. Strive hard to walk in the right path. One finds in it one's surest ally.

133. Right conduct ennobles one's family. Bad conduct makes one sink in the scale.

134. The Brahman may learn anew the Vedas which he forgot. If he were to fall from his estate he would be lost.

135. The envious do not prosper: likewise one straying from the right path does not advance.

136. The strong of mind will not shrink from virtue; for they know that any deviation is wrought with dire consequences.

137. Men of right conduct are crowned with glory. Men of evil ways are covered with disgrace.

138. Good conduct is the spring of happiness. Bad conduct leads one ever to misery.

139. It is difficult for a man of right conduct to utter evil words even in a forgetful mood.

140. Those who cannot move in harmony with the world are learned fools.

CHAPTER 15—PIṞAṈIL VIḺAIYĀMAI

141. Piṟaṉporuḷāḷ peṭṭoḻukum pētaimai jñālattu
aṟamporuḷ kaṇḍārkaṇ il.

142. Aṟaṉkaḍai niṉṟāruḷ ellām piṟaṉkaḍai
niṉṟāriṟ pedaiyār il.

143. Viḷintāriṉ vēṟallar maṉṟa teḷintāriṉ
tīmai purindoḻuku vār.

144. Eṉaittuṇaiya rāyiṉum eṉṉām tiṉaittuṇaiyum
tērāṉ piṟaṉil pukal.

145. Eḷiteṉa illiṟappāṉ eytum eñjñāṉṟum
viḷiyātu niṟkum paḻi.

146. Pakai pāvam accam paḻieṉa nāṉkum
ikavāvām illiṟappāṉ kaṇ.

147. Aṟaṉiyalāṉ ilvāḻvāṉ eṉbāṉ piṟaṉiyalāḷ
peṇmai nayavā tavaṉ.

148. Piṟaṉmaṉai nōkkāta pēṟāṇmai s'āṉṟōrkku
aṟaṉoṉṟō āṉṟa oḻukku.

149. Nalakkuriyār yāreṉiṉ nāmanīr vaippil
piṟaṟkuriyāḷ tōḷ tōyātār.

150. Aṟaṉvaraiyāṉ alla s'eyiṉum piṟaṉvaraiyāḷ
peṇmai nayavāmai naṉṟu.

CHAPTER 15—ON ADULTERY

141. The folly of intriguing with another's wife is not found in one versed in the laws of truth and wealth.

142. Among those who walk in the ways of sin, the most foolish are those who stand at the entrance of another's (house).

143. They are as good as dead who misbehave towards the wives of their confiding friends.

144. What avails one's greatness if one desecrates the sanctity of the house of another reckless of the consequences.

145. He who invades (easily) the house of another thinking it a mere trifle will incur eternal infamy.

146. Four evils, enmity, sin, fear and disgrace dog one who covets another's wife.

147. He is a true householder who does not love another man's wife.

148. The heroic manhood that does not lust after another's wife is to the wise not mere virtue but the very law of their being.

149. Verily he is a gentleman on this sea-girt earth who is free from the sin of adultery.

150. One may be guilty of any other sins; let one be free from adultery.

CHAPTER 16—POṞAIYUḌAIMAI

151. Akaḻvārait tāngum nilampōlat tammai
ikaḻvārp poṟuttal talai.

152. Poṟuttal iṟappiṉai eṉṟum ataṉai
maṟattal ataṉiṉum naṉṟu.

153. Iṉmaiyul iṉmai virundorāl : vaṉmaiyuḷ
vaṉmai maḍavārp poṟai.

154. Niṟaiyuṭaimai nīngāmai vēṇḍiṉ poṟaiuṭaimai
pōṟṟi oḻuka paṭum.

155. Oṟuttārai oṉṟāka vaiyārē vaippar
poṟuttāraip poṉpōl potindu.

156. Oṟuttārkku orunāḷai iṉbam : poṟuttārukkup
poṉṟun tuṇaiyum pukaḻ.

157. Tiṟanalla taṟpiṟar s'eyyiṉum nōnondu
aṟaṉalla s'eyyāmai naṉṟu.

158. Mikutiyāṉ mikkavai s'eydārait tāmtam
takutiyāṉ veṉṟu viḍal.

159. Tuṟandāriṉ tūymai uḍaiyar iṟandārvāy
iṉṉāccol nōṟkiṟ pavar.

160. Uṇṇātu nōṟpār periyar : piṟars'ollum
iṉṉāccol nōṟpāriṟ piṉ.

CHAPTER 16—ON PATIENCE

151. The earth sustains even those who dig into her. To bear with those who slander us is the crown of virtue.

152. Put up always with one's transgressions. Far greater than one's forbearance is one's oblivion of them.

153. Poverty within poverty is denying hospitality to guests; grace within grace is bearing with the foolish.

154. If one wishes to maintain character one's conduct must be marked by patience.

155. The world takes no note of the avenger but it esteems the patient like gold.

156. The delight of the avenger is for a day. The joy of the forbearing lasts till the end of the earth.

157. Resist not a wrong however grievous but forgive out of pity other's transgressions.

158. Conquer with forbearance one who has done you harm in one's insolent pride.

159. Greater than an ascetic is one who endures the insolent words of the transgressor.

160. Great are those who fast and do penance but greater than they are those who put up with insults.

CHAPTER 17—AḺUKKĀṞĀMAI

161. Oḻukkāṟāk koḷka oruvaṉtaṉ neñcattu
aḻukkāṟu ilāta iyalpu.

162. Viḻuppēṟṟiṉ ahtoppa tillaiyār māṭṭum
aḻukkāṟṟiṉ aṉmai peṟiṉ.

163. Aṟaṉākkam vēṇṭātāṉ eṉbāṉ piṟanākkam
pēṇātu aḻukkaṟup pāṉ.

164. Aḻukkāṟṟiṉ allavai s'eyyār iḻukkāṟṟiṉ
ētam paḍupākku aṟindu.

165. Aḻukkā ṟuḍaiyārkku atus'ālum oṉṉār
vaḻukkiyum kēṭīṉ padu.

166. Koḍuppadu aḻukkaṟuppāṉ s'uṟṟam uṭuppatūm
uṇpatūm iṉṟik keṭum.

167. Avvit taḻukkā ṟuṭaiyāṉaic ceyyavaḷ
tavvaiyaik kāṭṭi viḍum.

168. Aḻukkā ṟeṉavoru pāvi tiruccceṟṟut
tīyuḻi uyttu viḍum.

169. Avviyam neñcattāṉ ākkamum s'evviyāṉ
kēḍum niṉaikkap paṭum.

170. Aḻukkaṟṟu akaṉṟārum illai: ahtilār
perukkattiṉ tīrntārum il.

CHAPTER 17—ON ENVY

161. Let no one have envy; for freedom from envy must be one's virtue.

162. Envy none; there is no other possession greater than one's freedom from it.

163. He who envies other's riches neither loves virtue nor wealth.

164. The wise do not commit any wrong out of envy; for, they know the evils that spring from it.

165. The envious need no enemies to work their own ruin; for they find in their envy their sufficient foe.

166. The envious that stand in the way of charity perish with their kith and kin.

167. Fortune forsakes the envious to her elder sister.

168. Envy is a deadly sin. It blights one's fortune and casts one into hell.

169. The prosperity of the envious and the adversity of the virtuous afford food for reflection.

170. Envy never thrives; fortune never forsakes one who is free from it.

CHAPTER 18—VEHKĀMAI

171. Naḍuvinṟi naṉporul vehhiṉ kuḍipoṉṟik
kuṟṟamum ānkē tarum.

172. Paḍupayaṉ vehhip paḻippaḍuva s'eyyār
naḍuvaṉmai nāṇu pavar.

173. S'iṟṟiṉbam vehhı aṟaṉalla s'eyyārē
maṟṟiṉbam vēṇḍu pavar.

174. Ilameṉṟu vehkutal s'eyyār pulamveṉṟa
puṉmayil kāṭci yavar.

175. Ahki akaṉṟa aṟivueṉṉām yārmāṭṭum
vehki veṟiya s'eyiṉ.

176. Arulvehkı āṟṟiṉkaṉ nıṉṟāṉ porulvehkip
pollāta s'ūḻak keḍum.

177. Vēṇḍaṟka vehkiyām ākkam vilaivayiṉ
māṇḍaṟku aritām payaṉ.

178. Ahkāmai s'elvattıṟku yādeṉiṉ vehkāmai
vēṇḍum piṟaṉkaip porul.

179. Aṟaṉ aṟindu vehkā aṟivuḍaiyārc cērum
tiṟaṉaṟindu ānkē tiru.

180. Iṟalīṉum eṇṇātu vehkiṉ: viṟalīṉum
vēṇḍāmai eṉṉum s'erukku.

CHAPTER 18—ON NON-COVETING

171. Iniquitous coveting of wealth results in the ruin of one's home and brings in its train many sins.

172. Those who stand for equity do not commit sinful acts through covetousness.

173. Those who seek eternal happiness will never commit unrighteous acts through love of low pleasures.

174. The spotless wise who have conquered their senses, though destitute, will not covet other's wealth.

175. Of what avail is one's keen and penetrating intellect if one through covetousness acts foolishly?

176. Even he who treads the path of grace comes to ruin through covetous intentions.

177. Covet not other's wealth for out of covetousness spring evils.

178. Preservation of one's property lies through one's freedom from covetousness.

179. The wise who know what is righteous covet not: the Goddess of Fortune would seek them unbidden.

180. A blind covetousness brings about one's ruin. Freedom from it begets one's triumph.

CHAPTER 19—PUṞAN KŪRĀMAI

181. Aṟaṉkūṟāṉ alla s'eyiṉum oruvaṉ
puṟaṉ kūṟāṉ eṉṟal iṉitu.

182. Aṟaṉaḻī allavai s'eydaliṉ tītē
puṟaṉaḻi poyttu nakai.

183. Puṟankūṟip poyttuyır vāḻtaliṟ s'ādal
aṟankūṟum ākkam tarum.

184. Kaṇṇiṉṟu kaṇṇṟas' s'olliṉum s'ollaṟka
muṉṉiṉṟu piṉṉōkkāc col.

185. Aṟañcollum neñcattāṉ naṉmai puṟañcollum
puṉmaiyāṟ kāṇap paṭum.

186. Piṟaṉpaḻı kūṟuvāṉ taṉpaḻi yuḷḷum
tiṟanterindu kūṟap paṭum.

187. Pakaccolli kēḷirp pırippar nakaccolli
naṭpāṭal tēṟṟā tavar.

188. Tuṉṉiyār kuṟṟamum tūṟṟum maṟapiṉār
eṉṉaikol etilār māṭṭu.

189. Aṟaṉnōkki āṟṟumkol vaiyam puṟanōkkip
puṉs'ol uraippāṉ poṟai.

190. Etilār kuṟṟampōl tanguṟṟam kāṇkiṟpiṉ
tītuṇḍō maṉṉum uyirkku.

CHAPTER 19—ON NOT BACK-BITING

181. One may be guilty of wrongful deeds, but let not one be guilty of slander.

182. More heinous than sin is the deceitful smile of a slanderer.

183. Prefer death to a life of slander; for one finds in it the fruit of one's virtue.

184. Talk your bitterest to one's face but abstain from wanton slander.

185. The tongue of the base slanderer that talks of virtue belies his heart.

186. Ye scandal-mongers, beware of your being scandalized.

187. Those who alienate friends by back-biting may have forgotten the art of making friends through suavity of speech.

188. Those who trumpet the faults of their closest friends, what would they not do in the case of strangers?

189. How the earth bears the heavy burden of one who scandalises others! Perhaps patience is her virtue.

190. Will ever harm befall one who looks upon the faults of others as one's own?

CHAPTER 20—PAYAṈILA S'ŌLLĀMAI

191. Pallār muṉiyap payaṉila s'olluvāṉ
ellārum eḷḷap paṭum.

192. Payaṉila pallārmuṉ s'ollal nayaṉila
naṭṭārkaṇ s'eydaliṟ ṟītu.

193. Nayanilaṉ eṉbatu s'ollum payaṉila
pārit turaikkum urai.

194. Nayaṉs'ārā naṉmaiyiṉ nīnkum payaṉs'ārāp
paṇpils'ol pallār akattu.

195. S'īrmai s'iṟappoḍu nīnkum payaṉila
nīrmai uḍaiyār s'oliṉ.

196. Payaṉils'ol pārāṭṭu vāṉai makaṉeṉal
makkaṭ padaṭi yeṉal.

197. Nayaṉila s'olliṉum s'olluka s'āṉṟōr
payaṉila s'ollāmai naṉṟu.

198. Arumpayaṉ āyum aṟiviṉār s'ollār
perumpayaṉ illāta s'ol.

199. Poruḷtīrnda poccāndum s'ollār maruḷtīrnda
mās'aṟu kāṭci yavar.

200. S'olluka s'olliṟ payaṉuṭaiya: s'ollaṟka
s'oḷḷiṟ payaṉilāc col.

CHAPTER 20—ON FRIVOLITY OF SPEECH

191. He who revels in frivolous talk will be despised by all.

192. To talk frivolously in the presence of many is worse than an unjust act towards friends.

193. Indulgence in useless words at once betrays one's lack of probity.

194. Uttering empty words before all deprives one of one's sense of justice and mars one's noble qualities.

195. If good-natured men speak profitless words, their greatness and glory will disappear.

196. He is not a man but the chaff among men, who indulges in vain words.

197. Let great men speak untruth; it is better they refrain from uttering useless words.

198. Men of great discernment will never speak words devoid of great import.

199. Men of unclouded wisdom never utter nonsense even in a forgetful mood.

200. Speak profitable words; avoid nonsense.

CHAPTER 21—TĪVIṈAIYACCAM

201. Tīviṉaiyār añcār: viḻumiyār añcuvar:
tīviṉai yeṉṉum s'erukku.

202. Tīyavai tīya payattalāl tīyavai
tīyiṉum añcap paḍum.

203. Aṟiviṉuḷ ellān talaiyeṉba tīya
s'eṟuvārkkum s'eyyā viḍal.

204. Maṟandum piṟaṉkeṭu s'ūḻaṟka: s'ūḻiṉ
aṟams'ūḻum s'ūḻndavaṉ kēṭu.

205. Ilaṉeṉṟu tīyavai s'eyyaṟka: s'eyyiṉ
ilaṉākum maṟṟum peyarttu.

206. Tīppāla tāṉpiṟarkaṇ s'eyyaṟka: nōyppāla
taṉṉai aṭalvēṇḍā tāṉ.

207. Eṉaippakai uṟṟārum uyvar: viṉaippakai
vīyātu pins'eṉ ṟaṭum.

208. Tīyavai s'eytār keḍutal niḻaltaṉṉai
vīyā duḍiyuṟain daṟṟu.

209. Taṉṉaittāṉ kātalaṉ āyiṉ eṉaittoṉṟum
tuṉṉaṟka tīviṉaip pāl.

210. Arunkēṭaṉ eṉpatu aṟika marungōḍit
tīviṉai s'eyyāṉ eṉiṉ.

CHAPTER 21—ON FEAR OF EVIL DEEDS

201. Men hardened in sins do not fear evil; but the good dread it.

202. Evil is to be dreaded more than fire; for it lands one in disaster.

203. Not to return evil to those who do evil unto you, is, they say, the crown of wisdom.

204. Let none plot evil to others even in forgetfulness. If he does so, the God of Righteousness will compass his ruin.

205. Let none do wrong on account of poverty; if he does so he becomes poorer still.

206. Let not one do evil unto others, if one wants to be free from affliction.

207. You may escape your enemies but your evil follows you and hunts you down relentlessly.

208. Evil dogs you close on your heels like a shadow.

209. If one really loves oneself let one not do any harm to others.

210. Hardly doth sorrow befall one who does not deviate from right.

CHAPTER 22—OPPURAVAṞITAL

211. Kaimmāṟu vēṇḍā kaḍappāḍu mārimāṭṭu
eṉṉāṟṟun kollō ulaku.

212. Tāḷāṟṟit tanda poruḷellām takkārkku
vēḷāṇmai s'eytaṟ poruṭṭu.

213. Puttē ḷulakattum īṇḍum peṟalaritē
oppuraviṉ nalla piṟa.

214. Otta taṟivāṉ uyirvāḷvāṉ: maṟṟaiyāṉ
s'ettāruḷ vaikkap paḍum.

215. Ūruṇi nīrniṟain daṟṟē ulakavām
pēraṟi vāḷaṉ tiru.

216. Payaṉmaram uḷḷūrp paḻuttaṟṟāl s'elvam
nayaṉuḍai yāṉkaṇ paḍiṉ.

217. Maruntākit tappā marattaṟṟāl s'elvam
peruntakai yāṉkaṇ paḍiṉ.

218. Iḍaṉil paruvattum oppuraviṟ kolkār
kaḍaṉaṟi kāṭci yavar.

219. Nayaṉuḍaiyāṉ nalkūrndā ṉātal s'eyunīra
s'eyyādu amaikalā vāṟu.

220. Oppuravi ṉālvarum kēḍeniṉ ahdoruvaṉ
viṟṟukkōḷ takka duḍaittu.

CHAPTER 22—ON DECORUM

211. Do not expect any return for the services (duty) done. What does the world give in exchange for the clouds that pour rain?

212. All the wealth one earns is for rendering help to the deserving.

213. Is there anything greater than decorum either here or in the world to come?

214. Verily he is alive who is in harmony with the world; others should be ranked with the dead.

215. The wealth of the wise is a never-failing spring.

216. The wealth of the truly liberal is like a tree ripening in the heart of a village.

217. The wealth of the generous is like a healing medicinal tree.

218. Even in poverty the truly discerning never cease to be liberal.

219. The poverty of the liberal of heart is his failure in the offices of tenderness.

220. The poverty that results from a just course of action is worth purchasing by going into the very bond of slavery.

CHAPTER 23—ĪKAI

221. Vaṟiyārkkoṉ ṟīvatē īkai ; maṟ ṟellām
kuṟiyedirppai nīra duḍaittu.

222. Nallā ṟeṉiṉum koḷaltītu ; mēlulakam
illeṉiṉum ītalē naṉṟu.

223. Ilaṉeṉṉum evvam uraiyāmai ītal
kulaṉuḍaiyāṉ kaṇṇē uḷa.

224. Iṉṉā dirakkap paḍutal irantavar
iṉmukan kāṇum aḷavu.

225. Āṟṟuvār āṟṟal pas'iyāṟṟal : appas'iyai
māṟṟuvār āṟṟaliṟ piṉ.

226. Aṟṟār aḻipas'i tīrttal ahdoruvaṉ
peṟṟāṉ poruḷvaip paḻi.

227. Pāttūṇ marī yavaṉaip pas'iyeṉṉum
tīppiṇi tīṇḍal aritu.

228. Īttuvakkum iṉbam aṟiyārkol tāmuḍaimai
vaittiḻakkum vaṉka ṇavar.

229. Irattaliṉ iṉṉātu maṉṟa nirappiya
tāmē tamiyar uṇal.

230. S'ātaliṉ iṉṉāda dillai ; iṉiduatūm
ītal iyaiyāk kaḍai.

CHAPTER 23—ON LIBERALITY

221. Gift to the poor alone is true charity. Everything else is of the nature of a barter.

222. Receiving gifts is bad though one is assured of heaven. Bestowing gifts is good, though thereby one should be bereft of it.

223. The innately noble never beg but give ere charity begins.

224. Even to be begged is miserable for we feel wretched till the beggar's face is lit with joy.

225. Endurance of one's hunger is the test of one's penance. Far greater than that endurance is the spirit of appeasing the hunger of others.

226. Let the rich appease the devouring hunger of the indigent poor. It is a charity rendered unto themselves.

227. The pest of hunger never touches one who shares one's food with the poor.

228. The callous rich hide their barren metal; perhaps they know not the joy of giving.

229. More squalid than begging is a life of self-indulgence.

230. Death indeed is the greatest calamity; worse than death is one's failure in charity.

CHAPTER 24—PUGAḺ

231. Ītal is'aipaḍa vāḻtal aduvalladu
ūdiyam illai uyirkku.

232. Uraippār uraippavai yellām irappārkkoṉṟu
īvārmēl niṟkum pugaḻ.

233. Oṉṟā ulkat tuyarnda pugaḻallāl
poṉṟādu niṟpadoṉ ṟil.

234. Nilavarai nīḻpugaḻ āṟṟiṉ pulavaraip
pōṟṟātu puttēl ulaku.

235. Nattampōl kēḍum uḷatākum s'ākkāḍum
vittakark kallāl aritu.

236. Tōṉṟiṟ pugaḻoḍu tōṉṟuka : ahdilār
tōṉṟaliṟ ṟōṉṟāmai naṉṟu.

237. Pugaḻpaḍa vāḻātār tamnōvār ; tammai
igaḻvārai nōva devaṉ?

238. Vas'aiyeṉba vaiyattārk kellām is'aiyeṉṉum
eccam peṟāa viḍiṉ.

239. Vas'aiyilā vaṇpayaṉ kuṉṟum is'aiyilā
yākkai poṟutta nilam.

240. Vas'aiyoḻiya vāḻvārē vāḻvār is'aiyoḻiya
vāḻvārē vāḻā tavar.

END OF ILLARAVIYAL

CHAPTER 24—ON RENOWN

231. Give and make a name. There is no greater gain to man than such a renown.

232. The one undying theme of praise is the praise of charity.

233. Nothing lasts save one's fearless renown.

234. The wise are not favoured of the gods; but the renowned on earth are adored by them.

235. Out of death and ruin the wise fashion things enduring.

236. Let man be born to achieve renown. Let not the unrenowned see the light of day.

237. Let the inglorious blame themselves. Let them not reproach others.

238. World's reproach befalls one who does not achieve lasting fame.

239. In a land which bears the burden of the unrenowned even nature's bounty is on the wane.

240. The unblemished truly live; the unrenowned merely exist.

END OF THE SECTION ON DOMESTIC LIFE

TUṞAVAṞAVIYAL

CHAPTER 25—ARUḶUḌAIMAI

241. Aruṭcelvam s'elvattuṭ celvam : poruṭcelvam
pūriyār kaṇṇum uḷa.

242. Nallāṟṟāṉ nāḍi aruḷāḷka : pallāṟṟāl
tēriṉum ahdē tuṇai.

243. Aruḷs'ernda neñjiṉārk killai iruḷs'ērnda
iṉṉā ulakam pukal.

244. Maṉṉuyir ōmpi aruḷāḷvāṟ killeṉpa
taṉṉuyir añjum viṉai.

245. Allal aruḷāḷvārk killai vaḷivaḷangum
mallalmā ñālan kari.

246. Poruḷnīngip poccāndār enbar aruḷnīngi
allavai s'eydoḻuku vār.

247. Aruḷillārk kavvulakam illaip poruḷillārkku
ivvulakam illāki yāngu.

248. Poruḷaṟṟār pūppar orukāl; aruḷaṟṟār
aṟṟārmaṟ ṟātal aritu.

249. Teruḷātāṉ meypporuḷ kaṇḍaṟṟāl tēriṉ
aruḷātāṉ s'eyyum aṟam.

250. Valiyārmuṉ taṉṉai niṉaikka : tāṉtaṉṉiṉ
meliyārmēl s'ellum iḍattu.

III. ON RENUNCIATION

CHAPTER 25—ON COMPASSION

241. The crown of wealth is one's compassion; all other wealth is found even among meanest of men.

242. Be compassionate; for compassion is the pivot of all tenets.

243. The compassionate know not hell.

244. Freedom from dread of sin is only for the compassionate that love all creation.

245. The compassionate know not life's agonies: verily the wind-blown earth is witness to it.

246. The cruel that delight in sin perhaps know not what awaits them.

247. Heaven is not for the unfeeling; earth is not for the indigent.

248. Fortune may smile on the ruined; the unfeeling are the unredeemed.

249. Behold the unfeeling seeking virtue; it is like ignorance seeing light.

250. Oppress not the weak; remember your fate in stronger hands.

CHAPTER 26—PULĀL MAṞUTTAL

251. Taṉṉūṉ perukkaṟkut tāṉpiṟitūṉ uṇpāṉ
engaṉam āḷum aruḷ.

252. Poruḷāṭci pōṟṟātārk killai : aruḷāṭci
ānkillai ūṉtiṉ pavarku.

253. Paḍaikoṇḍār neñjampōl naṉṟūkkā doṉṟaṉ
uḍals'uvai uṇḍār maṉam.

254. Aruḷalladu yādeṉiṉ kollāmai kōṟal
poruḷalladu avvūṉ tiṉal.

255. Uṇṇāmai uḷḷatu uyirnilai : ūṉuṇṇa
aṇṇāttal s'eyyā taḷaṟu.

256. Tiṉaṟporuṭṭāl kollā dulakeṉiṉ yārum
vilaipporuṭṭāl ūṉtaruvār il.

257. Uṇṇāmai vēṇḍum pulāal piṟitoṉṟaṉ
puṇṇa duṉarvārp peṟiṉ.

258. S'eyiriṉ talaippirinda kāṭciyār uṇṇār
uyiriṉ talaippirinda ūṉ.

259. Avis'orindu āyiram vēṭṭaliṉ oṉṟaṉ
uyirs'ekuttu uṇṇāmai naṉṟu.

260. Kollāṉ pulālai maṟuttānaik kaikūppi
ellā uyirum toḷum.

CHAPTER 26—ON ABSTAINING FROM MEAT

251. He who fattens on the flesh of animals, can he ever understand the rule of love?

252. Wealth is not for the unwary. Compassion is not for the flesh-eater.

253. The heart of a flesh-eater is devoid of love like that of the wielder of a deadly weapon.

254. What is compassion but refraining from killing; what is sin but eating flesh?

255. Will there be throb of life when there is flesh-eating? Will there be any escape from hell for the flesh-eater?

256. Would there be meat for sale, if men were not to kill animals for eating flesh?

257. If one realises that meat is nothing but the wound of another creature, one refrains from eating it.

258. Men of clear vision abstain from the flesh of a slaughtered animal.

259. Far nobler than a thousand oblations on fire is an act of abstinence from flesh.

260. The whole world folds its hands in prayer to one who kills not and abjures flesh.

CHAPTER 27—TAVAM

261. Uṟṟanōy nōṉṟal uyirkkuṟukaṇ s'eyyāmai
aṟṟē tavattiṟk uru.

262. Tavamuṃ tavamuḍaiyārk kākum : avam ataṉai
ahdilār mēṟkoḷ vatu.

263. Tuṟandārkkut tuppuravu vēṇḍi maṟandārkol
maṟṟai yavarkaḷ tavam.

264. Oṉṉārt teṟalum uvantārai ākkalum
eṇṇiṉ tavattāṉ varum.

265. Vēṇḍiya vēṇḍiyāṅ geytalāl s'eytavam
īṇḍu muyalap paḍum.

266. Tavañceyvār tankarumam s'eyvār : maṟ ṟallār
avañceyvār ās'aiyuṭ paṭṭu.

267. S'uḍaccuḍarum poṉpōl oḷiviḍum tuṉbam
s'uḍaccuḍa nōṟkiṟ pavarkku.

268. Taṉṉuyir tāṉaṟap peṟṟāṉai ēṉaiya
maṉṉuyir ellām toḻum.

269. Kūṟṟan kudittalum kaikūḍum nōṟṟaliṉ
āṟṟal talaippaṭṭa varkku.

270. Ilarpalar ākiya kāraṇa nōṟpār
s'ilarpalar nōlā tavar

CHAPTER 27—ON PENANCE

261. The true form of penance is to put up with all pain and to abstain from injury.

262. Penance is possible only for the disciplined. Disgrace attends the undisciplined.

263. In their ministering to the needs of the ascetic, verily the householders have become oblivious of their penance.

264. Penance, if it wills can mar its foe, or bless its friend.

265. They persevere in penance; for through penance they achieve their desired goal.

266. To do penance is to be alive to one's duty; those enmeshed in desire come to ruin.

267. Gold shines all the more in fire; those who do penance become mellowed through suffering.

268. The world worships one who has regained one's soul.

269. Men at the height of their penance can triumph over even death.

270. Many are the indigent; for only a few practise penance.

CHAPTER 28—KŪḌĀ OḺUKKAM

271. Vañja maṉattāṉ paḍiṟṟoḷukkam pūtankaḷ
aindum akattē nakum.

272. Vāṉuyar tōṟṟam evaṉs'eyyum taṉṉeñcam
tāṉaṟi kuṟṟap paḍiṉ.

273. Valiyil nilaimaiyāṉ valluruvam peṟṟam
puliyiṉtōl pōrttumēyn daṟṟu.

274. Tavammaṟaindu allavai s'eytal putalmaṟaindu
vēṭṭuvaṉ puḷcimiḻt taṟṟu.

275. Paṟṟaṟṟēm eṉbār paḍiṟṟoḷukkam eṟṟeṟṟeṉṟu
ētam palavum tarum.

276. Neñjil tuṟavār tuṟandārpōl vañjittu
vāḻvāriṉ vaṉkaṇār il.

277. Puṟankuṉṟi kaṇḍaṉaiyar ēṉum akankuṉṟi
mūkkiṟ kariyār uḍaittu.

278. Maṉattatu mās'āka māṇḍār nīrāḍi
maṟaindoḻuku māndar palar.

279. Kaṇaikoḍitu yāḻkōḍu s'evvituāṉ kaṉṉa
viṉaipaḍu pālāl koḷal.

280. Maḻittalum nīṭṭalum vēṇḍā ulakam
paḻitta doḻittu viḍiṉ.

CHAPTER 28—ON IMPROPER CONDUCT

271. A man's five senses will laugh within at the false conduct of a deceitful mind.

272. Of what avail is a man's saintly mien, if his mind is bent on evil?

273. The ascetic appearance of one who has no strength of will, is like that of an ox grazing in the guise of a tiger.

274. Committing evil under the mask of holiness is like the hunter lying in wait for birds.

275. The hypocrisy of one who professes asceticism lands one in endless troubles.

276. There is none so hardened in vice as one who though hollow at heart, wears the mask of saintliness.

277. This world contains (many) men who like the Kunri seed are fair of face but foul of heart.

278. There are many insincere men who frequent sacred waters to pass for holy men.

279. The arrow, though straight is deadly; the yāḷ though crooked is sweet. Let people be judged by their actions.

280. If persons abstain from deeds condemned by the world there is no need either for tonsure or for matted locks.

CHAPTER 29—KAḶḶĀMAI

281. Eḷḷāmai vēṇḍuvāṉ eṉbāṉ eṉaittoṉṟum
kaḷḷāmai kākkataṉ neñcu.

282. Uḷḷattāl uḷḷalum tītē piṟaṉporuḷaik
kaḷḷattāl kaḷvēm eṉal.

283. Kaḷaviṉāl ākiya ākkam aḷaviṟandu
āvadu pōlak keḍum.

284. Kaḷaviṉkaṇ kaṉṟiya kātal viḷaiviṉkaṇ
vīyā viḻumam tarum.

285. Aruḷkaruti aṉbuḍaiyar ātal poruḷkarutip
poccāppup pārppārkaṇ il.

286. Aḷaviṉkaṇ niṉṟuoḻukal āṟṟār kaḷaviṉkaṇ
kaṉṟiya kāta lavar.

287. Kaḷaveṉṉum kār aṟivu āṇmai aḷaveṉṉum
āṟṟal purindārkaṇ il.

288. Aḷavaṟindār neñjat taṟampōla niṟkum
kaḷavaṟindār neñjiṟ karavu.

289. Aḷavalla s'eytānkē vīvar kaḷavalla
maṟṟaiya tēṟṟā tavar.

290. Kaḷvārkkut taḷḷum uyirnilai kaḷḷārkkut
taḷḷātu puttē ḷulaku.

CHAPTER 29—ON NON-STEALING

281. He who wants to command respect must guard his mind against robbing others.

282. It is a sin to lust for another's belongings.

283. Ill-gotten wealth however vast comes to nought.

284. Inordinate desire to steal brings in its train endless suffering.

285. Can ever grace and love be found in one who exploits the unwary.

286. Those who have a burning desire to steal cannot walk in the path of virtue.

287. The dark thought of stealing is absent in those who are alive to the value of life.

288. Virtue dwells in the person of known probity; deceit dwells in persons addicted to stealing.

289. Those who know nothing else than stealing will indulge in unrighteous acts and forthwith perish.

290. Their very bodies fail the defrauding. The world of the gods fail not the upright.

CHAPTER 30—VĀYMAI

291. Vāymai eṉappaḍuvadu yādeṉiṉ yādoṉṟum
tīmai yilāta s'olal.

292. Poymmaiyum vāymai iḍatta puraitīrnda
naṉmai payakkum eṉiṉ.

293. Taṉneñ jaṟivadu poyyaṟka : poyttapiṉ
taṉneñjē taṉṉaic cuḍum.

294. Uḷḷattāl poyyā doḻukiṉ ulakattār
uḷḷattuḷ ellām uḷaṉ.

295. Maṉattoḍu vāymai moḻiyiṉ tavattoḍu
dāṉañcey vāriṉ talai.

296. Poyyāmai yaṉṉa pugaḻillai : eyyāmai
ellā aṟamum tarum.

297. Poyyāmai poyyāmai āṟṟiṉ aṟampiṟa
s'eyyāmai s'eyyāmai naṉṟu.

298. Puṟantūymai nīrāṉ amaiyum : akantūymai
vāymaiyāṟ kāṇap paḍum.

299. Ellā viḷakkum viḷakkalla : s'āṉṟōrkkup
poyyā viḷakkē viḷakku.

300. Yāmmeyyāk kaṇḍavaṟṟuḷ illai eṉaittoṉṟum
vāymaiyiṉ nalla piṟa.

CHAPTER 30—ON TRUTH

291. What is truth but unsullied utterance?

292. Even untruth has the stamp of truth, if it is free from harm.

293. Let none utter a falsehood against his conscience lest it should torment him.

294. One sits high in the hearts of all who is true to oneself.

295. Far greater than a benefactor or an ascetic is one whose words come from the depths of truth.

296. One's renown is rooted only in truth; it leads one easily to every other virtue.

297. Practise truth, you need not practise any other virtue.

298. Water cleanses the body; truth cleanses the soul.

299. All lamps are not lamps. To the great the lamp of truth is the lamp.

300. In all the scriptures we have read, there is no virtue greater than truth.

CHAPTER 31—VEKUḶĀMAI

301. S'elliḍattuk kāppāṉ s'iṉankāppāṉ : alliḍattuk
kākkiṉeṉ kāvākkāl eṉ.

302. S'ellā iḍattuc ciṉantītu : s'elliḍattum
illataṉiṉ tīya piṟa.

303. Maṟattal vekuḷiyai yārmāṭṭum tīya
piṟattal ataṉāṉ varum.

304. Nakaiyum uvakaiyum kolluñ ciṉattiṉ
pakaiyum uḷavō piṟa.

305. Taṉṉaittāṉ kākkiṉ s'iṉankākka : kāvākkāl
taṉṉaiyē kollum s'iṉam.

306. S'iṉameṉṉum s'ērndāraik kolli iṉameṉṉum
ēmap puṇaiyaic cuḍum.

307. S'iṉattaip poruḷeṉṟu koṇḍavaṉ kēḍu
nilattaṟaindāṉ kaipiḷaiyā daṟṟu.

308. Iṇareri tōyvaṉṉa iṉṉā s'eyiṉum
puṇariṉ vekuḷāmai naṉṟu.

309. Uḷḷiya ellām uḍaṉeytum uḷḷattāl
uḷḷāṉ vekuḷi eṉiṉ.

310. Iṟandār iṟandār aṉaiyar : s'iṉattait
tuṟandār tuṟandār tuṇai.

CHAPTER 31—ON NOT GETTING ANGRY

301. He who restrains his wrath where it can be vented shows real restraint. What does it matter whether one restrains it or not in an unavailing hour?

302. Anger is bad even where it is unavailing; but where it can be effectively exercised there is no worse evil.

303. Do not get angry with any one; for out of anger springs forth a host of evils.

304. Is there any enemy other than anger that kills both joy and pleasure?

305. If a man were to guard himself let him restrain anger. Otherwise anger gets the better of him.

306. Anger destroys even one's kindred who is the canoe of his life.

307. The ruin of one who nourishes wrath is as certain as the injury to one's hands when beat on the ground.

308. It is better you show no wrath even against one who inflicts on you harm scorching you like a thousand-tongued flame.

309. Banish anger from your mind; you get all that you long for.

310. Men given to wrath are one with the devil; Men free from it are one with the immortals.

CHAPTER 32—I<u>N</u><u>N</u>ĀS'EYYĀMAI

311. S'iṟappīṉuñ celvam peṟiṉum piṟarkkiṉṉā
s'eyyāmai mās'aṟṟār kōḷ.

312. Kaṟuttiṉṉā s'eytavak kaṇṇum maṟuttiṉṉā
s'eyyāmai mās'aṟṟār kōḷ.

313. S'eyyāmaṟ ceṟṟārkkum iṉṉāda s'eytapiṉ
uyyā viḻumam tarum.

314. Iṉṉās'ey tārai oṟuttal avarnāṇa
naṉṉayañ ceytu viḍal.

315. Aṟiviṉāṉ ākuva duṇḍō piṟitiṉnōy
tannōypōl pōṟṟāk kaḍai.

316. Iṉṉā eṉattāṉ uṇarntavai tuṉṉāmai
vēṇḍum piṟaṉkaṇ s'eyal.

317. Eṉaittāṉum eññāṉṟum yārkkum maṉattāṉām
māṇāccey yāmai talai.

318. Taṉṉuyirk kiṉṉāmai tāṉaṟivāṉ eṉkolō
maṉṉuyirk kiṉṉā s'eyal.

319. Piṟarkkiṉṉā muṟpakal s'eyyiṉ tamakkiṉṉā
piṟpakal tāmē varum.

320. Nōyellām nōys'eytār mēlavām : nōy s'eyyār
nōyiṉmai vēṇḍu pavar,

CHAPTER 32—ON NOT DOING EVIL

311. It is the nature of the spotless not to inflict suffering on others, though by it they may get wealth and renown.

312. It is the nature of the stainless not to resist evil.

313. Even our vengeance for a wanton injury results in our own unbearable sorrow.

314. The noblest revenge is to put the foe to the blush by our acts of kindness.

315. What profiteth one's reason, if one does not feel others, sufferings as his own and guard against them ?

316. Avoid all that causes pain to others.

317. It is the supremest virtue not to commit at any time even slight injury to others.

318. How is it a man inflicts injury upon others knowing how painful it would be to himself?

319. As the night follows day, evil that we do recoils on us.

320. All sufferings befall those who inflict harm on others. Those who desire immunity from suffering never commit injury.

CHAPTER 33—KOLLĀMAI

321. Aṛaviṉai yāteṉil kollāmai: kōṛal
piṛaviṉai yellām tarum.

322. Pakuttuṇḍu palluyir ōmbutal nūlōr
tokuttavaṟṟuḷ ellām talai.

323. Oṉṛāka nallatu kollāmai: maṟṟataṉ
piṉs'ārap poyyāmai naṉṛu.

324. Nallā ṛeṉappaḍuvadu yādeṉiṉ yādoṉṛum
kollāmai s'ūḻum neṛi.

325. Nilaiyañji nīttārul ellām kolaiyañjik
kollāmai s'ūḻvāṉ talai.

326. Kollāmai mēṛkoṇ doḻukuvāṉ vāḻnāḷmēl
s'ellādu uyiruṇṇum kūṛṛu.

327. Taṉṉuyir nīppiṉum s'eyyaṛka tāṉpiṛi
tiṉṉuyir nīkkum viṉai.

328. Naṉṛākum ākkam perideṉiṉum s'āṉṛōrkkuk
koṉṛākum ākkam kaḍai.

329. Kolaiviṉaiyar ākiya mākkaḷ pulaiviṉaiyar
puṉmai terivār akattu.

330. Uyiruḍambiṉ nīkkiyār eṉbar s'eyiruḍambiṉ
s'ellātti vāḻkkai yavar.

CHAPTER 33—NOT KILLING

321. If you ask what is the sum total of virtues, it is non-killing; killing begets sin.

322. All the scriptures emphasise the virtue of hospitality and the creed of non-violence.

323. The crown of all virtues is non-violence. Next comes non-lying.

324. The path of rectitude is the path of non-violence.

325. Far greater than an ascetic who renounces the fleeting world is the follower of non-violence.

326. Yama, the Destroyer of life, never invades the realm where non-violence prevails.

327. Do not commit any act of violence though your life is in peril.

328. The truly great scorn the riches acquired through slaughter.

329. In the eyes of the discerning, men given to slaughter are but churls.

330. Behold the Lazarus, he is guilty of acts of violence in his former birth,

CHAPTER 34—NILAIYĀMAI

331. Nillāta vaṟṟai nilaiyiṉa eṉṟuṇarum
pullaṟi vāṇmai kaḍai.

332. Kūttāṭ ṭavaikkuḻāt taṟṟē : peruñcelvam
pōkkum atuviḷin daṟṟu.

333. Aṟkā iyalpiṟṟuc celvam : atupeṟṟāl
aṟkupa āṅkē s'eyal.

334. Nāḷeṉa oṉṟupōl kāṭṭi uyirīrum
vāḷa tuṇarvārp peṟiṉ.

335. Nācceṟṟu vikkuḷmēl vārāmuṉ nalviṉai
mēṟceṉṟu s'eyyap paḍum.

336. Nerunal uḷaṉoruvaṉ iṉṟillai eṉṉum
perumai uḍaittiv vulaku.

337. Orupoḻutum vāḻva daṟiyār karutupa
kōṭiyum alla pala.

338. Kuḍambai taṉittoḻiyap puḷpaṟan daṟṟē
uḍamboḍu uyiriḍai naṭpu.

339. Uṟanguvatu pōlum s'ākkāḍu uṟangi
viḻippatu pōlum piṟappu.

340. Pukkil amaintiṉṟu kollō uḍambiṉuḷ
tuccil irunda uyirkku.

CHAPTER 34—INSTABILITY

331. It is contemptible folly to mistake the unstable for the stable.

332. The flow of fortune is like the gathering of a crowd at a concert; its ebb is like the melting of the crowd at its close.

333. Fortune is fickle; if you come by it delay not; put it to proper use.

334. Time seems all laughter; but to the discerning it is a saw sawing away the life of men.

335. Before hiccough arises and before the tongue is paralysed do good that leads to salvation.

336. Yesterday he was but to-day he is not; this is the glory of the earth.

337. One is not sure what awaits him the next moment; but he becomes a prey to a thousand and one thoughts.

338. The attachment of life to the body is like that of a full-fledged bird flying from its broken shell.

339. Death is like sleep, birth is that awakening from sleep.

340. Why should the soul seek a temporary shelter in the perishable body? Is there not a durable habitation for it?

CHAPTER 35—TUṞAVU

341. Yātaṉiṉ yātaṉiṉ nīngiyāṉ nōtal
ataṉiṉ ataṉiṉ ilaṉ.

342. Vēṇḍiṉuṇ ḍākat tuṟakka tuṟandapiṉ
īṇḍiyaṟ pāla pala.

343. Aḍalvēṇḍum aintaṉ pulattai : viḍalvēṇḍum
vēṇḍiya vellām orunku.

344. Iyalpākum nōṉbiṟkoṉ ṟiṉmai uḍaimai
mayalākum maṟṟum peyarttu.

345. Maṟṟum toḍarppāḍu evaṉkol piṟappaṟukkal
uṟṟārk kuḍambum mikai.

346. Yāṉeṉa deṉṉum s'erukkaṟuppāṉ vāṉōrkku
uyarnda ulakam pukum.

347. Paṟṟi viḍāa iḍumbaikaḷ paṟṟiṉaip
paṟṟi viḍāa tavarkku.

348. Talaippaṭṭār tīrat tuṟandār mayanki
valaippaṭṭār maṟṟai yavar.

349. Paṟṟaṟṟa kaṇṇē piṟappaṟukkum maṟṟu
nilaiyāmai kāṇap paḍum.

350. Paṟṟuka paṟṟaṟṟāṉ paṟṟiṉai : appaṟṟaip
paṟṟuka paṟṟu viḍaṟku.

CHAPTER 35—RENUNCIATION

341. A man does not suffer pain from whatever things he has renounced.

342. There is endless joy in early renunciation.

343. Subdue your senses and give up all your longings.

344. Renunciation is the mark of asceticism. Any clinging leads to one's delusion.

345. Why talk of other attachments; even our body is a hindrance.

346. He enters the abode of the gods who lays the axe at 'I' and 'mine.'

347. Sufferings seize men of desire.

348. Salvation is for one of renunciation; others get entangled in endless births and deaths.

349. Cut off all attachments; you cut off the tangle of life; otherwise you are caught.

350. Cling fast to Him who is free from all desire. Seek Him for your freedom from attachment.

CHAPTER 36—MEYYUṆARTAL

351. Poruḷalla vaṟṟaip poruḷeṉ ṟuṇarum
maruḷāṉām māṇāp piṟappu.

352. Iruḷnīngi iṉbam payakkum maruḷnīngi
mās'aṟu kāṭci yavarkku.

353. Aiyattiṉ nīngit teḷindārkku vaiyattiṉ
vāṉam naṇiyadu uḍaittu.

354. Aiyuṇarvu eydiak kaṇṇum payamiṉṟē
meyyuṇarvu illā davarkku.

355. Epporuḷ ettaṉmait tāyiṉum apporuḷ
meypporuḷ kāṇpa daṟivu.

356. Kaṟṟīṇḍu meypporuḷ kaṇḍār talaippaḍuvar
maṟṟīṇḍu vārā neṟi.

357. Ōrttuḷḷam uḷḷatu uṇariṉ orutalaiyāp
pērttuḷḷa vēṇḍā piṟappu.

358. Piṟappeṉṉum pētaimai nīngac ciṟappeṉṉum
s'emporuḷ kāṇpa daṟivu.

359. S'ārpuṇarndu s'ārpu keḍaoḷukiṉ maṟṟaḻittuc
cārtarā s'ārtarum nōy.

360. Kāmam vekuḷi mayakkam ivai mūṉṟaṉ
nāmam keḍakkeḍu nōy.

CHAPTER 36—TRUE KNOWLEDGE

351. Out of ignorance which mistakes things unreal for things real springs the wretched cycle of births.

352. Men of pure vision are led from darkness to light.

353. To men of unclouded wisdom heaven is nearer than earth.

354. What profits one's perfect senses if one is not endowed with true knowledge.

355. To track all things to their subtlest retreats is true knowledge.

356. Those who have learnt the truth never enter back to this world.

357. There is no fear of one's re-birth if one seeks and finds the truth.

358. Seek the truth to remove delusion; that is wisdom.

359. Seek the truth on which everything rests; you will be free from all the ills that assail life.

360. Wipe out the very names of lust, anger and delusion; you will be wiping out the cause of re-birth.

CHAPTER 37—AVĀVAṞUTTAL

361. Avāveṉpa ellā uyirkkum eññāṉṟum
tavāap piṟappīṉum vittu.

362. Vēṇḍunkāl vēṇḍum piṟavāmai : maṟṟatu
vēṇḍāmai vēṇḍa varum.

363. Vēṇḍāmai yaṉṉa viḻuccelvam īṇḍillai :
yāṇḍum ahdoppa dil.

364. Tūuymai eṉpadu avāiṉmai : maṟṟatu
vāaymai vēṇḍa varum.

365. Aṟṟavar eṉbār avāaṟṟār : maṟṟaiyār
aṟṟāka aṟṟa dilar.

366. Añjuva tōrum aṟaṉē oruvaṉai
vañjippa dōrum avā.

367. Avāviṉai āṟṟa aṟuppiṉ tavāviṉai
tāṉvēṇḍum āṟṟāṉ varum.

368. Avā illārkkillākum tuṉbam : ahduṇḍēl
tavāadu mēṉmēl varum.

369. Iṉbam iḍaiyaṟātu īṇḍum avāveṉṉum
tuṉbattuṉ tuṉban keḍiṉ.

370. Ārā iyaṟkai avānīppiṉ annilaiyē
pērā iyaṟkai tarum.

CHAPTER 37—THE DESTRUCTION OF DESIRE

361. The learned say desire is the eternal seed of life.

362. Do you long for anything? Long for not being born again; this you can achieve if you cease your desires.

363. There is no greater possession than freedom from desire either here or in the world beyond.

364. What is purity of mind but absence of desire? It will follow if one burns for truth.

365. Only those who have renounced are free; others are not.

366. It is desire that seduces men into sin; Asceticism dreads desires.

367. The desired path of virtue is open to one who kills desire.

368. There is no sorrow for those who are free from desire. Endless sorrows befall men with desire.

369. There is an eternal flow of life's happiness when desire, the evil of all evils, dies out.

370. Give up your insatiable longings; you will be conferring on yourself an eternal life.

CHAPTER 38—ŪḺ

371. Ākūḷāl tōṉṟum as'aiviṉmai kaipporuḷ:
pōkūḷāl tōṉṟum maḍi.

372. Pēdaip paḍukkum iḻavūḻ: aṟivakaṟṟum
ākalūḻ uṟṟak kaḍai.

373. Nuṇṇiya nūlpala kaṟpiṉum maṟṟumtaṉ
uṇmai aṟivē mikum.

374. Iruvēṟu ulakat tiyaṟkai: tiruvēṟu:
teḷḷiyar ātalum vēṟu.

375. Nallavai ellām tīyavām: tīyavum
nallavām s'elvañ ceyaṟku.

376. Pariyiṉum ākāvām pālalla uyttuc
coriyiṉum pōkā tama.

377. Vakuttāṉ vakutta vakaiyallāl kōti
tokuttārkkum tuyttal aritu.

378. Tuṟappārmaṉ tuppura villār uṟaṟpāla
ūṭṭā kaḻiyum eṉiṉ.

379. Naṉṟānkāl nallavāk kāṇpavar aṉṟānkāl
allaṟ paḍuva devaṉ.

380. Ūḻiṟ peruvali yāvuḷa: maṟṟoṉṟu
s'ūḻiṉum tāṉmun duṟum.

END OF AṞATTUPPĀL

CHAPTER 38—FATE

371. Out of fate springs perseverence which leads to one's fortune. Out of fate springs one's indolence which leads to one's ruin.

372. Fate makes fools of the wise. Fate makes folly pass for wisdom.

373. What if one is a man of subtle learning: one's mind is swayed by fate.

374. Fate has a double sway. It makes the foolish rich and the wise poor.

375. Things favourable become adverse, and the unfavourable favourable.

376. One may lose one's wealth however carefully one may guard it. One may not lose it though he flings it away. It is all ordained by fate.

377. Unless pre-ordained by the divine Disposer, even if a man did pile up a crore it would not be possible for him to enjoy it.

378. The poor could easily renounce the world if fate were to refrain from visiting them with the curse of their past deeds.

379. Why worry about pain and pleasure? They are all the workings of fate.

380. What is there so potent as Fate? Even if we devise some way of counteracting it, it takes us by surprise.

END OF AṚATTUPPĀḶ

PORUṬPĀL

CHAPTER 39—IṞAIMĀṬCI

381. Paḍaikuḍi kūḻamaiccu naṭparaṉ āṟum
uḍaiyāṉ aras'aruḷ ēṟu.

382. Añjāmai īkai aṟivūkkam innāṉkum
eñjāmai vēndaṟku iyalpu.

383. Tūngāmai kalvi tuṇivuḍaimai immūṉṟum
nīngā nilaṉāḷ pavaṟku.

384. Aṟaṉiḻukkādu allavai nīkki maṟaṉiḻukkā
māṉa muḍaiyadu aras'u.

385. Iyaṟṟalum īṭṭalum kāttalum kātta
vakuttalum valla daras'u.

386. Kāṭcik keḷiyaṉ kaḍuñcollaṉ allaṉēl
mīkkūṟum maṉṉaṉ nilam.

387. Iṉs'olāl īttaḷikka vallāṟkut taṉs'olāl
tāṉkaṇḍa aṉaittiv vulaku.

388. Muṟais'eydu kāppāṟṟum maṉṉavaṉ makkaṭku
iṟaiyeṉṟu vaikkap paḍum.

389. S'evikaippac coṟpoṟukkum paṇbuḍai vēndaṉ
kavikaikkīḻt tangum ulaku.

390. Koḍaiaḷi s'enkōl kuḍiyōmpal nāṉkum
uḍaiyāṉām vēndarkku oḷi.

SECTION I. THE STATE

CHAPTER 39—ON MAJESTY

381. He is a lion among kings, who possesses with an army, a territory, wealth, ministers, allies and a fortress.

382. Fearlessness, liberality, wisdom and energy are the unfailing marks of a King.

383. The ruler of the earth must never be bereft of his sleepless watchfulness, learning and courage.

384. He is an honourable King who swerves not from virtue and abstains from vice.

385. He is the King who is capable of acquiring, preserving and wisely distributing wealth.

386. The world will extol the kingdom of one who is easy of access and who does not indulge in harsh words.

387. He who is not harsh of tongue but full of grace and liberality commands the homage of the world.

388. He is a God among men who shields his subjects.

389. The world is under the sway of the monarch who puts up with bitter counsel.

390. He is a light among Kings who is endowed with liberality, grace, love for his subjects, and a desire for just rule.

CHAPTER 40—KALVI

391. Kaṟka kas'aḍaṟak kaṟpavai: kaṟṟapiṉ
niṟka ataṟkut taka.

392. Eṇṇeṉpa ēṉai eḻutteṉpa ivviraṇḍum
kaṇṇeṉpa vāḻum uyirkku.

393. Kaṇṇuḍaiyar eṉpavar kaṟṟōr: mukattiraṇḍu
puṇṇuḍaiyar kallā tavar.

394. Uvappat talaikkūḍi uḷḷap pirital
aṉaittē pulavar toḻil.

395. Uḍaiyārmuṉ illārpōl ēkkaṟṟum kaṟṟār:
kaḍaiyarē kallā tavar.

396. Toṭṭaṉaittu ūṟum maṇaṟkēṇi: māndarkkuk
kaṟṟaṉait tūṟum aṟivu.

397. Yādāṉum nāḍāmal ūrāmāl eṉṉoruvaṉ
s'āntuṇaiyum kallāda vāṟu.

398. Orumaikkaṇ tāṉkaṟṟa kalvi oruvaṟku
eḻumaiyum ēmāppu uḍaittu.

399. Tāmiṉ puṟuvatu ulakiṉ puṟakkaṇḍu
kāmuṟuvar kaṟṟaṟin tār.

400. Kēḍil viḻuccelvam kalvi oruvaṟku
māḍualla maṟṟai yavai.

CHAPTER 40—ON LEARNING

391. Faultlessly pursue knowledge and abide by it.

392. Verily the numbers and letters are the eyes of the living one.

393. The learned alone are said to possess eyes; but they are only sores in the face of the unlettered.

394. The duty of the learned is to delight man by their company. Hunger ever more for it even while parting.

395. Eager like the beggars at the door of the wealthy is the sufferer of knowledge; the illiterate are held in scorn.

396. The deeper you delve into the earth, the greater will be the flow of water. Likewise knowledge is in proportion to your learning.

397. No country and no place is alien to the learned. How is it that persons remain in ignorance to the end of their lives?

398. The knowledge that a person gains in one birth stands him in good stead for seven births.

399. The learned thirst for knowledge more and more, because what gives them pleasure, delights the world.

400. The precious undecaying wealth of a man is his learning. All other riches are no wealth at all.

CHAPTER 41—KALLĀMAI

401. Aranginṟi vaṭṭāḍi yaṟṟē nirampiya
nūlinṟik kōṭṭi koḷal.

402. Kallādāṉ s'oṟkā muṟutal mulaiyiraṇḍum
illādāḷ peṇkāmuṟ ṟaṟṟu.

403. Kallā tavarum naṉinallar kaṟṟārmuṉ
s'ollā dirukkap peṟiṉ.

404. Kallādāṉ oṭpam kaḻiyanaṉ ṟāyiṉum
koḷḷār aṟivuḍai yār.

405. Kallā oruvaṉ takaimai talaippeydu
s'ollāḍac cōrvu paḍum.

406. Uḷareṉṉum māttiraiyar allāl payavāk
kaḷaraṉaiyar kallā tavar.

407. Nuṇmāṇ nuḻaipulam illāṉ eḻilnalam
maṇmāṇ puṉaipāvai yaṟṟu.

408. Nallārkaṇ paṭṭa vaṟumaiyiṉ iṉṉātē
kallārkaṇ paṭṭa tiru.

409. Mēṟpiṟandār āyiṉum kallādār kīḻppiṟandum
kaṟṟār aṉaittilar pāḍu.

410. Vilangoḍu makkaḷ aṉaiyar ilangunūl
kaṟṟārōḍu ēṉai yavar.

CHAPTER 41—ON NON-LEARNING

401. Entering an assembly without sufficient knowledge is like playing at a dice board without its knowledge.

402. The desire of the ignorant to speak is like the desire of a woman without breasts claiming womanhood.

403. Blessed are the ignorant if they venture not to address the assembly of the learned.

404. The learned value not the intelligence of the illiterate.

405. The pretensions of the illiterate disappear the moment they launch upon a discussion with the learned.

406. The ignorant just exist; they are like a piece of barren land.

407. The imposing position of one who lacks penetrating intellect reminds us of the external glitter of clay.

408. Far sweeter is the poverty of the learned than the riches of the ignorant.

409. The highborn ignorant sink low in the scale while the learned even of humble birth are exalted.

410. The ignorant are but beasts by the side of men of wide learning.

CHAPTER 42—KĒḶVI

411. S'elvattuḷ s'elvam s'eviccelvam accelvam
s'elvattuḷ ellām talai.

412. S'evikkuṇavu illāda pōḻdu s'iṟitu
vayiṟṟukkum īyap paḍum.

413. S'eviyuṇavin kēḷvi yuḍaiyār aviyuṇavin
āṉṟārōḍu oppar nilattu.

414. Kaṟṟilan āyinum kēṭka : ahdoruvaṟku
oṟkattin ūṟṟām tuṇai

415. Iḻukkal uḍaiyuḻi ūṟṟukkōl aṟṟē
oḻukkam uḍaiyārvāyc col.

416. Eṉaittāṉum nallavai kēṭka : aṉaittāṉum
āṉṟa perumai tarum.

417. Piḻaittuṇarndum pēdaimai s'ollār iḻaittuṇarndu
īṇḍiya kēḷvi yavar.

418. Kēṭpiṉum kēḷāt takaiyavē kēḷviāl
tōṭkap paḍāta s'evi.

419. Nuṇangiya kēḷviyar allār vaṇangiya
vāyiṉar ātal aritu.

420. S'eviyin s'uvaiuṇarā vāyunarvin mākkal
aviyiṉum vāḻiṉum eṉ.

CHAPTER 42—ON HEARING

411. The wealth of all wealth is the wealth of hearing. It outtops all other wealth.

412. Men think a little of the stomach only when the ear is not fed.

413. Those mortals who feast their ears with learning are one with the immortals with their sacrificial offerings.

414. Though devoid of learning let one fill one's ear with knowledge. It is his prop in his hour of gloom.

415. The counsel of the upright is like a staff over a slippery ground.

416. Listen to wholesome counsel however meagre; for out of it springs great good.

417. Men of searching understanding do not speak foolishly even in a thoughtless mood.

418. The ear that is not filled with understanding is really deaf.

419. Men that lack subtle understanding lack modesty in speech.

420. What avails it whether men live or die, if they merely satisfy the palate and not feed the ear with wisdom.

CHAPTER 43—AṞIVUḌAIMAI

421. Aṟivu aṟṟam kākkum karuvi: s'eṟuvārkkum
uḷaḻikkal ākā araṇ.

422. S'eṉṟa iḍattāl s'elaviṭāt tītuorīi
naṉṟiṉpāl uyppatu aṟivu.

423. Epporuḷ yāryārvāyk kēṭpiṉum apporuḷ
meypporuḷ kāṇpa taṟivu.

424. Eṇporuḷa vākac celaccollit tāṉpiṟarvāy
nuṇporuḷ kāṇpa taṟivu.

425. Ulakaṉ taḻīiyatu oṭpam : malartalum
kūmpalum illadu aṟivu.

426. Evvatu uṟaivadu ulakam ulakattōḍu
avvatu uṟaivadu aṟivu.

427. Aṟivuḍaiyār āvatu aṟivār: aṟivilār
ahdaṟi kallā tavar.

428. Añjuvadu añjāmai pētaimai: añjuvadu
añjal aṟivār toḻil.

429. Ediradāk kākkum aṟiviṉārkku illai
adira varuvadōr nōy.

430. Aṟivuḍaiyār ellām uḍaiyār: aṟivilār
eṉṉuḍaiya rēṉum ilar.

CHAPTER 43—ON KNOWLEDGE

421. The weapon of wisdom saves one from evil. It is a citadel which cannot be destroyed by the foe.

422. Wisdom bridles the wandering mind, keeps it away from evil and bids it tread the right path.

423. Wisdom seeks the truth of all things which are heard or uttered.

424. Wisdom unravels things subtle and seeks them in others.

425. To befriend the world is wisdom; and wisdom is not inconstant like the flower that blossoms and fades.

426. To be one with the world is wisdom.

427. Wisdom knows the future but not ignorance.

428. It is folly not to fear what must be feared. It is wisdom to fear what must be feared.

429. Men of foresight who guard themselves against coming events know no distress.

430. The wise possess everything; but the poor are the unwise rich.

CHAPTER 44—KUṞṞAM KAṬITAL

431. S'erukkum s'iṉamum s'iṟumaiyum illār
perukkam perumita nīrttu.

432. Ivaṟalum māṇpiṟanta māṉamum māṇā
uvakaiyum ētam iṟaikku.

433. Tiṉaittuṇaiyām kuṟṟam variṉum paṉaittuṇaiyāk
koḷvar paḻināṇu vār.

434. Kuṟṟamē kākka poruḷākak kuṟṟamē
aṟṟam tarūum pakai.

435. Varumuṉṉark kāvātāṉ vāḻkkai erimuṉṉar
vaittūṟu pōlak keḍum.

436. Taṉkuṟṟam nīkkip piṟarkuṟṟam kāṇkiṟpiṉ
eṉkuṟṟam ākum iṟaikku.

437. S'eyaṟpāla s'eyyātu ivaṟiyāṉ s'elvam
uyaṟpāla taṉṟik keḍum.

438. Paṟṟuḷḷam eṉṉum ivaṟaṉmai eṟṟuḷḷum
eṇṇap paḍuvatoṉṟu aṉṟu.

439. Viyavaṟka eññāṉṟum taṉṉai : nayavaṟka
naṉṟi payavā viṉai.

440. Kātala kātal aṟiyāmai uykkiṟpiṉ
ētila ētilār nūl.

CHAPTER 44—ON RESTRAINING FAULTS

431. Exalted is the wealth that is free from pride, wrath and lust.

432. Niggardliness, empty honour, blind favouritism, are all the faults of a King.

433. Even the slightest fault looms large in the eyes of those who dread dishonour.

434. Guard against your error as you would your wealth. For error spells your ruin.

435. Like a piece of straw in a consuming flame, will be destroyed the life of one who does not guard against faults.

436. What fault will befall a King who is free from guilt and detects guilt in others ?

437. The hoarded wealth of the miser who fails in his offices perishes.

438. A clutching greedy heart that knows no charity commits the greatest folly.

439. Let not conceit enter your heart at any time of your life ; do not run after trifles.

440. Of what avail are the designs of the foe, if one does not betray one's secrets ?

CHAPTER 45—PERIYĀRAIT TUṆAIKKŌṬAL

441. Aṟaṉaṟintu mūtta aṟivuḍaiyār kēṇmai
tiṟaṉaṟintu tērndu koḷal.

442. Uṟṟanōy nīkki uṟāamai muṉkākkum
peṟṟiyārp pēṇik koḷal.

443. Ariyavaṟṟuḷ ellām aritē periyāraip
pēṇit tamarāk koḷal.

444. Tammiṟ periyār tamarā oḻukutal
vaṉmaiyuḷ ellām talai.

445. S'ūḻvārkaṇ ṇāka oḻukalāṉ maṉṉavaṉ
s'ūḻvāraic cūḻntu koḷal.

446. Takkār iṉattaṉāyt tāṉoḻuka vallāṉaic
ceṟṟār s'eyakkiṭandatu il.

447. Iḍikkum tuṇaiyārai āḷvārai yārē
keḍukkum takaimai yavar.

448. Iḍippārai illāda ēmarā maṉṉaṉ
keḍuppār ilāṉum keḍum.

449. Mutalilārkku ūtiyam illai : matalaiyām
s'ārpilārkku illai nilai.

450. Pallār pakaikoḷaliṉ pattaḍutta tımaittē
nallār toḍarkai viṭal.

CHAPTER 45—ON ASSOCIATION WITH ELDERS

441. The friendship of virtuous men of mature wisdom is to be appreciated and secured.

442. Seek the friendship of those who can remove existing distress and guard against future.

443. To seek and win the alliance of the great is the rarest of all blessings.

444. To follow in the footsteps of those that are greater than oneself is the crown of one's strength.

445. Verily the ministers are the eyes of the monarch ; let the monarch have tried ones.

446. No adversary can ruin the King who relies on his efficient counsellors.

447. None can harm the ruler who seeks the wholesome counsel of his ministers though bitter.

448. The King who is not guarded by men of firm counsel will perish even though he has no enemies.

449. Is there profit without capital ? Is there security for the monarch devoid of wise counsellors ?

450. Greatly injurious is the forsaking of the friendship of the good ; it is like encountering single-handed many foes.

CHAPTER 46—S'IṞṞIṈAṄ CĒRĀMAI

451. S'iṛṛiṉam añjum perumai: s'iṟumaitāṉ
s'uṛṛamāc cūḻndu viṭum.

452. Nilattiyalpāṉ nīrtirin daṛṛākum: māndarkku
iṉattiyalpu aduākum aṟivu.

453. Maṉattāṉām māndarkku uṇarcci; iṉattāṉām
iṉṉāṉ eṉappaḍum col.

454. Maṉattuḷatu pōlak kāṭṭi oruvaṛku
iṉattuḷatu ākum aṟivu.

455. Maṉantūymai s'eyviṉai tūymai iraṇḍum
iṉantūymai tūvā varum.

456. Maṉamtūyārku eccamnaṉ ṟākum: iṉamtūyārkku
illainaṉ ṟākā viṉai.

457. Maṉanalam maṉṉuyirkku ākkam: iṉanalam
ellāp pukaḻum tarum.

458. Maṉanalam naṉkuḍaiya rāyiṉum s'āṉṟōrkku
iṉanalam ēmāp puḍaittu.

459. Maṉanalattiṉ ākum maṟumai: maṟ ṟahdum
iṉanalattiṉ ēmāppu uḍaittu.

460. Nalliṉattiṉ ūnkun tuṇaiyillai: tīyiṉattiṉ
allaṟ paḍuppatūum il.

CHAPTER 46—ON AVOIDING LOW COMPANY

451. The great dread the company of the ignoble, for the ignoble delight in the company of the mean.

452. Water smacks of the soil; The wisdom of man takes the colour of the company he keeps.

453. It is the mind that helps a man to gain knowledge: but it is one's association that makes people say what sort of man he is.

454. One's wisdom partakes of the nature of one's mind and one is known by the company he keeps.

455. Purity of mind and purity of action are of a piece with the purity of one's associates.

456. A good progeny awaits the pure. There is no effort of one endowed with good company but bears fruit.

457. Company of the pure brings one all glory.

458. The wise may be pure in mind. Good company is the source of one's strength.

459. Heaven awaits the pure of heart; verily it is the reward of good company.

460. There is no greater evil than the company of the wicked,

CHAPTER 47—TERINDU S'EYAL VAKAI

461. Aḻivatūum āvatūum āki vaḻipayakkum
ūtiyamum s'ūḻntu s'eyal.

462. Terinda iṉattoḍu tērndeṇṇic ceyvārkku
arumporuḷ yātoṉṟum il.

463. Ākkam karuti mutaliḻakkum s'eyviṉai
ūkkār aṟivuḍaiyār.

464. Teḷivi lataṉait toḍankār iḷiveṉṉum
ētappāḍu añju pavar.

465. Vakaiyaṟac cūḻāḍu eḻutal pakaivaraip
pāttip paḍuppadōr āṟu.

466. S'eytakka alla s'eyakkeḍum : s'eytakka
S'eyyāmai yāṉum keḍum.

467. Eṇṇit tuṇika karumam : tuṇindapiṉ
eṇṇuvam eṉbadu iḻukku.

468. Āṟṟiṉ varundā varuttam palarniṉṟu
pōṟṟiṉum pottup paḍum.

469. Naṉṟāṟṟa luḷḷun tavaṟuṇḍu : avaravar
paṇbaṟindu āṟṟāk kaḍai.

470. Eḷḷāta eṇṇic ceyalvēṇḍum ; tammoḍu
koḷḷāda koḷḷādu ulaku.

CH. 47—ON ACTION AFTER DUE DELIBERATION

461. After much deliberation over profit and loss and the final gains, launch on a task.

462. Nothing is impossible for those who act after listening to the counsel of persons of known probity.

463. The wise do not approve of the action of those who lose their capital anticipating some distant gain.

464. Men who dread ignominy never embark on a work without deliberation.

465. A thoughtless expedition only fosters the might of one's foes.

466. To do a thing which ought not to be done is to court trouble; to fail to do a thing which ought to be done is to land oneself in ruin.

467. Begin your task after much deliberation. To think after launching action is to court a grievous blunder.

468. An ill-organised scheme though supported by many goes to pieces.

469. Even a good scheme falls through if we do not divine aright the disposition of men.

470. Let not the king do any unwise act lest the world should hold him in scorn.

CHAPTER 48—VALIYAṞITAL

471. Viṉaivaliyum taṉvaliyum māṟṟāṉ valiyum
tuṇaivaliyum tūkkic ceyal.

472. Olvatu aṟivatu aṟintataṉ kaṇtangic
celvārkkuc cellādadu il.

473. Uḍaittam valiaṟiyār ūkkattiṉ ūkki
iḍaikkaṇ murindār palar.

474. Amaindāngu oḻukāṉ aḷavaṟiyāṉ taṉṉai
viyandāṉ viraindu keḍum.

475. Pīlipey s'ākāṭum accuiṟum appaṇḍam
s'āla mikuttup peyiṉ.

476. Nuṉikkombar ēṟiṉār ahdiṟandu ūkkiṉ
uyirkkiṟuti āki viṭum.

477. Āṟṟiṉ aḷavaṟindu īka: atuporuḷ
pōṟṟi vaḻanku neṟi.

478. Āku āṟu aḷaviṭṭitu āyiṉum kēḍillai
Pōku āṟu akalāk kaḍai.

479. Aḷavaṟindu vāḻātāṉ vāḻkkai uḷapōla
illākit tōṉṟāk keḍum.

480. Uḷavarai tūkkāta oppuravu āṇmai
vaḷavarai vallaik keḍum.

CH. 48—ON KNOWING THE ENEMY'S STRENGTH

471. A king must act after measuring the strength of his plan, his own resources, the strength of the enemy and that of the ally.

472. Nothing is impossible for them who know the nature of their task and throw themselves heart and soul into it.

473. Many kings have failed in the middle of their enterprise, for they have launched on it in their blind ignorant zeal.

474. He who is ignorant of the might of his foe and who thinks too much of himself will come to grief.

475. The axle of a cart breaks even under the overload of a peacock's feathers.

476. Over-vaulting ambition perishes.

477. Let your charity be according to the measure of your wealth. That is the way to preserve it.

478. No harm comes of one's small earnings. Let not one's expense out-run one's income.

479. The seeming prosperity of the extravagant perishes.

480. The fortune of one, lavish of charity beyond measure, goes to rack and ruin.

CHAPTER 49—KĀLAM AṚITAL

481. Pakalvellum kūkaiyaik kākkai : ikalvellum
vēndarkku vēṇḍum poḻudu.

482. Paruvattō ḍoṭṭa oḻukal tiruviṉait
tīrāmai ārkkum kayiṛu.

483. Aruviṉai eṉba uḷavō karuviyāl
kālam aṛindu s'eyiṉ.

484. Ṅālan karuttinum kaikūḍum kālam
karuti iḍattāṛ s'eyiṉ.

485. Kālan karuti iruppar kalankātu
ñālan karutu pavar.

486. Ukkam uḍaiyāṉ oḍukkam porutakar
tākkaṛkup pērum takaittu.

487. Poḷḷeṉa ānkē puṛamvērār kālampārttu
uḷvērppar oḷḷi yavar.

488. S'eṛunaraik kāṇiṉ s'umakka : iṛuvarai
kāṇiṉ kiḻakkām talai.

489. Eytaṛ kariyaduḷiyaintakkāl annilaiyē
s'eytaṛ kariya s'eyal.

490. Kokkokka kūmpum paruvattu : maṛṛataṉ
kuttokka s'īrtta iḍattu.

CHAPTER 49—ON KNOWING THE TIME

481. During the day the crow conquers the owl. So the monarch who wishes to defeat the enemy must choose the proper time.

482. Action at the appropriate hour is the rope that holds for ever the Goddess of Fortune to the King.

483. Is there anything impossible if one acts at the right time and with the proper equipment?

484. One can succeed in the attempt to conquer the world if the right time and the right place are chosen.

485. He who without any fear aims at the conquest of the world will await the season for it.

486. The self-restraint of the mighty is like the drawing back of the fighting ram just before its attack.

487. The wise will not fly into a passion when assailed; they allow their anger to smoulder within till the right time comes.

488. Bow before the enemy till the time of his destruction. When the hour comes, strike him down.

489. Do not let slip a golden opportunity; when the hour dawns, attempt the impossible.

490. When the time is not ripe, be still as a heron. But at the ripe hour, attack the enemy without missing your aim.

CHAPTER 50—IḌAṈ AṚITAL

491. Toḍangaṛka evviṉaiyum eḷḷaṛka muṟṟum
iḍankaṇḍa piṉṉal latu.

492. Muraṇs'ernta moymbi ṉavarkkum araṇs'erndām
ākkam palavum tarum.

493. Āṟṟārum āṟṟi aḍupa : iḍaṉaṛindu
pōṟṟārkaṇ pōṟṟic ceyiṉ.

494. Eṇṇiyār eṇṇam iḻappar iḍaṉaṛindu
tuṉṉiyār tuṉṉic ceyiṉ.

495. Neḍumpuṉaluḷ vellum mutalai : aḍumpuṉaliṉ
nīngiṉ ataṉaip piṛa.

496. Kaḍalōḍā kālval neḍunter kaḍalōḍu
nāvāyum ōḍā nilattu.

497. Añjāmai allāl tuṇaivēṇḍā eñjāmai
eṇṇi iḍattāṉ s'eyiṉ.

498. S'iṛupaḍaiyāṉ s'eliḍam s'eriṉ uṛupaḍaiyāṉ
ūkkam aḻindu viḍum.

499. S'iṛainalaṉum s'īrum ilareṉīṉum māndar
uṛainilattōḍu oṭṭal aritu.

500. Kālāḻ kaḷariṉ nariaḍum kaṇañjā
vēlāḷ mukatta kaḷiṟu.

CHAPTER 50—ON KNOWING THE PLACE

491. Scorn not the foe; embark not on any action till you secure a coign of vantage to overwhelm him.

492. Even to men of great valour and power, manifold are the advantages yielded by a fortress.

493. Even the weak are able to win if they choose the right place to assail the foe.

494. If a king stations himself at a right place the conquering foe loses all hope.

495. The crocodile in waters deep overpowers all; once it leaves the waters, he falls an easy prey to its foes.

496. The strong wheeled lofty chariot cannot cross the seas, nor can ocean sailing ships move on land.

497. If one selects a suitable place by one's discretion, no other help is needed.

498. Ruined will be the strength of one who takes a large army to a place where the enemy of small forces is entrenched.

499. A people may not have either strength or strongholds; still it is difficult to fight with them on their own soil.

500. A mad elephant that kills the bold spearman is killed even by a jackal when it gets stuck up in the mire.

CHAPTER 51—TERINDU TEḶITAL

501. Aṛamporuḷ iṉbam uyiraccam nāṉkiṉ
tiṛamterindu tēṛap paḍum.

502. Kuḍippiṛandu kuṛṛattiṉ nīngi vaḍuppariyum
nāṇuḍaiyāṉ kaṭṭē teḷivu.

503. Ariyakaṛṛu ās'aṛṛār kaṇṇum teriyunkāl
iṉmai aritē veḷiṛu.

504. Guṇanāḍik kuṛṛamum nāḍi avaṛṛuḷ
mikaināḍi mikka koḷal.

505. Perumaikkum ēṉaic ciṛumaikkum tattam
karumamē kaṭṭaḷaik kal.

506. Aṛṛārait tēṛutal ōmpuka: maṛṛavar
paṛṛilar nāṇār paḻi.

507. Kātaṉmai kandā aṛivaṛiyārt teṛutal
pēdaimai ellān tarum.

508. Tērāṉ piṛaṉait teḷindāṉ vaḻimuṛai
tīrā iḍumbai tarum.

509. Tēṛaṛka yāraiyum tērātu: tērndapiṉ
tēṛuka tēṛum poruḷ.

510. Tērāṉ teḷivum teḷiṉdāṉkaṇ aiyuṛavum
tīrā iḍumbai tarum.

CH. 51—ENGAGING SERVANTS AFTER TEST

501. One should be chosen after putting one to a fourfold test of righteousness, wealth, inclination and fear of life and death.

502. One of good family, free of faults, and possessed of a wholesome fear of sin, should be chosen.

503. One may be an unblemished man and of vast learning: but it is rare to find one free from ignorance.

504. Examine the good and bad in a person and judge his character according to what predominates in his composition.

505. One's own deed is the touchstone of one's greatness and littleness.

506. Choose not persons who have no kith and kin, and who possess : no social instincts, they will be callous of heart and dread no crime.

507. It is the height of folly to choose the ignorant blinded by affection.

508. To choose a stranger without knowing his traits results in one's grief.

509. Let men be chosen with deliberate care; when once the choice is made, let no suspicions crump into your soul.

510. To choose men with no forethought and to suspect them will land you in endless woes.

CHAPTER 52—TERINDU VIṈAIYĀṬAL

511. Naṉmaiyum tīmaiyum nāḍi nalampurinda
taṉmaiyāṉ āḷap paḍum.

512. Vāri perukki vaḷampaṭuttu uṟṟavai
ārāyvāṉ s'eyka viṉai.

513. Aṉpaṟivu tēṟṟam avāiṉmai iṉṉānkum
naṉkuḍaiyāṉ kaṭṭē teḷivu.

514. Eṉaivakaiyāl tēṟiyak kaṇṇum viṉaivakaiyāṉ
vēṟākum māndar palar.

515. Aṟindāṟṟic ceykiṟpāṟku allāl viṉaitāṉ
s'iṟandāṉeṉṟu ēvaṟpāṟ ṟaṉṟu.

516. S'eyvāṉai nāḍi viṉaināḍik kālattōḍu
eyda uṇarndu s'eyal.

517. Idaṉai idaṉāl ivaṉmudikkum eṉṟāyndu
adaṉai avaṉkaṇ viḍal.

518. Viṉaikkurimai nāḍiya piṉṟai avaṉai
ataṟkuriya ṉākac ceyal.

519. Viṉaikkaṇ viṇaiyuḍaiyāṉ kēṇmaivē ṟāka
niṉaippāṉai nīngum tiru.

520. Nāḍōṟum nāḍuka maṉṉaṉ viṉais'eyvāṉ
kōḍāmai kōḍādu ulaku.

CH. 52—ON APPOINTMENT ACCORDING TO MERIT

511. After examining the good and the bad, cling to the good.

512. He who taps all productive sources and guards against losses is the true servant.

513. Choose men, who are endowed with love, wisdom, clever vision and freedom from covetousness.

514. Position corrupts even the men of our own deliberate choice.

515. Let worth prevail. Let not blind affection dictate the choice of men.

516. The thing to be done, the proper person for it and the appropriate time for doing it, must all be duly weighed.

517. Let the king be first convinced of the competency of a person ; then he shall allow him to move freely in the sphere of his appointed task.

518. Choose men of approved merit and then make them worthy of the station.

519. Prosperity deserts one who suspects the motives of a servant ever loyal to his work.

520. Let them not swerve from the right path ; for on them rests the just conduct of the world.

CHAPTER 53—S'UṞṞANTAḺĀL

521. Paṟṟaṟṟa kaṉṉum paḻamaipā rāṭṭutal
s'uṟṟattār kaṇṇē uḷa.

522. Viruppaṟāc cuṟṟam iyaiyiṉ aruppaṟā
ākkam palavun tarum.

523. Aḷavaḷāvu illātāṉ vāḻkkai kuḷavaḷāk
kōḍiṉṟi nīrniṟain daṟṟu.

524. S'uṟṟattāl s'uṟṟap paḍaoḻukal s'elvantāṉ
peṟṟattāl peṟṟa payaṉ.

525. Koḍuttalum iṉs'olum āṟṟiṉ aḍukkiya
s'uṟṟattāl s'uṟṟap paḍum.

526. Perunkoḍaiyāṉ pēṇāṉ vekuḷi avaṉiṉ
marunkuḍaiyār mānilattu il.

527. Kākkai karavāk karaintuṇṇum : ākkamum
aṉṉanī rārkkē uḷa.

528. Podunōkkāṉ vēndaṉ varis'aiyā nōkkiṉ
adunōkki vāḻvār palar.

529. Tamarākit taṟṟuṟantār s'uṟṟam amarāmaik
kāraṇam iṉṟi varum.

530. Uḻaippirindu kāraṇattiṉ vandāṉai vēndaṉ
iḻaittirundu eṇṇik koḷal.

CHAPTER 53—ON CHERISHING ONE'S KINDRED

521. It is one's own kith and kin that cherish their old attachments to men out of suit with fortune.

522. One's unceasing kinship is the source of all one's fourtune.

523. The life of one with no kin will be like overflowing waters of a tank with no bund.

524. The value of one's wealth consists in a life surrounded by one's kinsmen.

525. One delights in the company of one generous of heart and suave of speech.

526. Nothing excels on earth the love of one large of heart and free of wrath, but shares it with the rest.

527. Fortune smiles on one of like disposition.

528. The king must not be indifferent to one's deserts but reward people according to their merit.

529. Reject none on the score of disagreement. Men who have become estranged will flock to you.

530. Let the king embrace his estranged kith and kin by redressing their grievances.

CHAPTER 54—POCCĀVĀMAI

531. Iṛanta vekuḷiyiṉ tītē s'iṛanda
uvakai makiḻcciyiṉ s'ōrvu.

532. Poccāppuk kollum pukaḻai aṛiviṉai
nicca nirappukkoṉ ṛānku.

533. Poccāppārk killai pukaḻmai atuulakattu
eppālnū lōrkkun tuṇivu.

534. Accam uḍaiyārk karaṇillai : āngillai
poccāp puḍaiyārkku naṉku.

535. Muṉṉuṛak kāvādu iḻukkiyāṉ taṉpiḻai
piṉṉūṛu irangi viḍum.

536. Iḻukkāmai yārmāṭṭum eṉrum vaḻukkāmai
vāyiṉ atuoppa dil.

537. Ariya eṉṛu ākāta illaipoc cāvāk
karuviyāl pōṟṟic ceyiṉ.

538. Pukaḻntavai pōṟṟic ceyalvēṇḍum : s'eyyātu
ikaḻntārkku eḻumaiyum il.

539. Ikaḻcciyiṟ keṭṭārai uḷḷuka tāmtam
makiḻcciyiṉ mainturum pōḻtu.

540. Uḷḷiyatu eytal eḷitumaṉ maṟṟumtāṉ
uḷḷiyatu uḷḷap peṟiṉ.

CHAPTER 54—AGAINST FORGETFULNESS

531. Forgetfulness which cometh of mad joy is more dangerous than wild wrath.

532. Poverty freezes knowledge. Forgetfulness blights one's reputation.

533. Fame is not for the thoughtless, so say the scriptures of the world.

534. Of what avail is a citadel to a crown, what good availeth the thoughtless.

535. Who is not on his guard against impending evil, rues his folly.

536. There is no greater good than to be ever on the vigil.

537. Nothing is impossible for the thoughtful.

538. No good awaits him in birth to come who fails of his noble deeds.

539. When drunk with delight, remember those who have perished through wilful neglect.

540. No task is difficult to the thoughtful and diligent,

CHAPTER 55—S'ENKŌṈMAI

541. Ōrntukaṉ ṉōḍādu iṟaipurindu yārmāṭṭum
tērndus'ey vaḥdē muṟai.

542. Vāṉōkki vāḻum ulakellām : maṉṉavaṉ
kōṉōkki vāḻum kuḍi.

543. Antaṉar nūṟkum aṟattiṟkum ādiyāy
niṉṟatu maṉṉavaṉ kōl.

544. Kuḻitaḻīik kōlōccu mānila maṉṉaṉ
aḍitaḻīi niṟkum ulaku.

545. Iyalpuḷik kōlōccu maṉṉavaṉ nāṭṭa
peyalum viḷaiyuḷum tokku.

546. Vēlaṉṟu veṉṟi taruvatu: maṉṉavaṉ
kōlatūum kōṭādu eṉiṉ.

547. Iṟaikākkum vaiyakam ellām : avaṉai
muṟaikākkum muṭṭāc ceyiṉ.

548. Eṉpadattāṉ orā muṟais'eyyā maṉṉavaṉ
taṉpadattāl tāṉē keḍum. ,

549. Kuḍipuṟan kāttōmbik kuṟṟan kaḍital
vaḍuvaṉṟu vēndaṉ toḻil.

550. Kolaiyiṟ koḍiyārai vēndoṟuttal, painkūḻ
kaḷaikaṭ ṭataṉoḍu ṉer.

CHAPTER 55—ON RIGHTEOUS SCEPTRE

541. Strict enquiry, and impartial justice mark the rule of a just monarch.

542. The world looks to rain for its existence. The subjects look to the sceptre for their existence.

543. The king's sceptre is the standing proof of Brahminical books and their teachings.

544. The world falls at the feet of a great King who wields the sceptre for his subjects' welfare.

545. Both seasonal rains and waving corn are seen in the land of a righteous monarch.

546. Victory is won not by the spear but by the unswerving sceptre of a monarch.

547. The king protects the whole world and justice protects him if unfailingly admonished.

548. The king who does not administer impartial justice goes to ruin.

549. To punish crime is the duty, not the fault of the king who attends to the welfare of his subjects.

550. Punishing murderers with death is like plucking out weeds among the crops.

CHAPTER 56—KOḌUNKŌṈMAI

551. Kolaimēṟ koṇḍāril koḍitē alaimēṟkoṇḍu
allavai s'eytoḷukum vēndu.

552. Vēloḍu ninṟān iḍuenṟatu pōlum
kōloḍu ninṟān iravu.

553. Nāḍoṟum nāḍi muṟais'eyyā mannavan
nāḍoṟum nāḍu keḍum.

554. Kūḷun kuḍiyum orunkiḷakkum kōlkōḍic
cūḷātu s'eyyum aras'u.

555. Allaṟpaṭ ṭāṟṟādu aḷudakan nīranṟē
s'elvattait tēykkum paḍai.

556. Mannarkku mannutal s'enkōnmai ; ahdinṟēl
mannāvām mannarkku oḷi.

557. Tuḷiinmai ñālattiṟku eṟṟaṟṟē vēndan
aḷiinmai vāḷum uyirkku.

558. Inmaiyin innādu uḍaimai muṟais'eyyā
mannavan kōṟkīḻp paḍin.

559. Muṟaikōḍi mannavan s'eyyin uṟaikōḍi
ollātu vānam peyal.

560. Āpayan kunṟum ; aṟutoḷilor nūlmaṟappar ;
kāvalan kāvān enin.

CHAPTER 56—ON UNRIGHTEOUS RULE

551. The unrighteous king who oppresses his subjects is more cruel than the one who leads the life of a murderer.

552. The wielder of the sceptre asking for gifts, is like the spearman asking the way-farer 'give.'

553. That country will perish any day whose monarch does not administer justice day by day.

554. That king who allows his sceptre to bend indiscriminately will lose his wealth together with his subjects.

555. Are not the tears, shed as a result of oppression, the weapons which destroy the prosperity of the monarch ?

556. Good Government makes one's rule enduring. Where it is not found, his lustre will not last long.

557. The people who live under a graceless king suffer like the earth unvisited by drops of rain.

558. Where people possess a king, who does not enforce justice, wealth does not confer more happiness than poverty.

559. Were the king to rule unjustly, the Heavens would withhold rains.

560. If the protecting monarch fails in his duties, the yield of cows will diminish and Brahmans with their six duties will forget their Vedas.

CHAPTER 57—VERUVANTA S'EYYĀMAI

561. Takkānku nāḍit talaiccellā vaṉṉattāl
ottāngu oṟuppatu vēndu.

562. Kaṭitōcci mella. eṟika ; neḍituākkam
nīngāmai vēṇḍu pavar.

563. Veruvanta s'eytoḻukum venkōlaṉ āyiṉ
oruvantam ollaik keḍum.

564. Iṟaikaṭiyaṉ eṉṟuraikkum iṉṉāccol vēndaṉ
uṟaikaḍuki ollaik keḍum.

565. Aruñcevvi iṉṉā mukattāṉ peruñcelvam
pēeykaṇḍu aṉṉadu uḍaittu.

566. Kaḍuñcollaṉ kaṇṇilaṉ āyiṉ neḍuñcelvam
nīḍiṉṟi ānkē keḍum.

567. Kaḍumoḻiyum kaiyikanda ṭaṇḍamum vēndaṉ
aḍumuraṇ tēykkum aram.

568. Iṉattāṟṟi eṇṇāda vēndaṉ s'iṉattāṟṟic
cīṟiṉ s'iṟukum tiru.

569. S'eruvanda pōḻtiṉ s'iṟais'eyyā vēndaṉ
veruvandu veytu keḍum.

570. Kallārp piṇikkum kaḍunkōl ; atuvalladu
illai nilakkup poṟai.

CHAPTER 57—ON TYRANNY

561. A righteous king investigates and fittingly punishes the wrongdoer so that he may not repeat it.

562. If you wish enduring prosperity behave as if you punish excessively, but do it mildly.

563. The tyrant who terrifies his subjects will soon perish.

564. That king whom people speak of as a tyrant will rapidly perish.

565. The great wealth of a king who is inaccessible and assumes a fearful look, is no better than in the possession of a demon.

566. The abundant wealth of a king who utters harsh words and puts on unkind looks will not last long.

567. Severity in speech and excess in punishment are like the file which removes his capacity to destroy (his enemies).

568. The prosperity of a king who does not consult his advisers but makes them the victims of his fury will shrink.

569. If a king who has no fortress meets a foe, he will be ruined by fear.

570. No burden is harder for the earth to bear than the cruel sceptre wielded by the unwise.

CHAPTER 58—KAṆṆŌṬṬAM

571. Kaṇṇōṭṭam eṉṉum kaḻiperun kārikai
uṇmaiyāṉ uṇḍuiv vulaku.

572. Kaṇṇōṭṭattu uḷḷadu ulakiyal ; ahdilār
uṇmai nilakkup poṟai.

573. Paṇeṉām pāḍaṟku iyaipuiṉṟēl ; kaṇeṉṉām
kaṇṇōṭṭam illāta kaṇ.

574. Uḷapōl mukattevaṉ s'eyyum aḷaviṉāl
kaṇṇōṭṭam illāta kaṇ.

575. Kaṇṇiṟku aṇikalam kaṇṇōṭṭam ahdiṉṟēl
puṇṇeṉṟu uṇarap paḍum.

576. Maṇṇōḍu iyainda marattaṉaiyar kaṇṇōḍu
iyandukaṇ ṇōḍa tavar.

577. Kaṇṇōṭṭam illavar kaṇṇilar ; kaṇṇuḍaiyār
kaṇṇōṭṭam iṉmaiyum il.

578. Karumam s'itaiyāmal kaṇṇōḍa vallārkku
urimai yuḍaittiv vulaku.

579. Oṟuttāṟṟum paṇpiṉār kaṇṇumkaṇ ṇōḍip
poṟuttāṟṟum paṇpē talai.

580. Peyakkaṇḍu naññuṇḍu amaivar nayattakka
nākarikam vēṇḍu pavar.

CHAPTER 58—ON KINDLINESS

571. The world exists because of the existence of the most beautiful virtue called kindliness.

572. The world lives through kindliness; those who do not have it are a burden to the earth.

573. What is the use of a song that could not be enjoyed? Likewise, what is the use of the eyes that have no kindliness?

574. What is the use of one's eyes if they do not beam with immeasurable love?

575. Kindliness is the fitting ornament for the eyes. They are a sore, where it is absent.

576. Those whose eyes do not reflect love resemble trees that stand on the earth.

577. Verily they are blind who have no kindly look.

578. The world belongs to a king who can do his duty and yet be courteous.

579. It behoves a king to put up with the doer of harm and even be kind to him.

580. Those who wish to acquire loveable urbanity will knowingly swallow even the poison served.

CHAPTER 59—OṞṞĀṬAL

581. Oṟṟum uraisānṟa nūlum ivaiiranḍum,
teṟṟenka mannavan kaṇ.

582. Ellārkkum ellām nikaḻpavai eññānṟum
vallaṟital vēndan toḻil.

583. Oṟṟinān oṟṟip poruḷteriyā mannavan
koṟṟam koḷakkiḍandadu il.

584. Vinais'eyvār tañcuṟṟam vēṇḍātār enṟānku
anaivaraiyum ārāyvadu oṟṟu.

585. Kaḍāa uruvoḍu kaṇṇaññjādu yāṇḍum
ukāamai vallatē oṟṟu.

586. Tuṟantār paḍivattar āki iṟandārāyndu
ens'eyinum s'ōrviladu oṟṟu.

587. Maṟaintavai kēṭkavaṟṟāki aṟintavai
aiyappāḍu illatē oṟṟu.

588. Oṟṟoṟṟit tanta poruḷaiyum maṟṟumōr
oṟṟināl oṟṟik koḷal.

589. Oṟṟoṟṟu uṇarāmai āḷka; uṭanmūvar
s'oṟṟokka tēṟap paḍum.

590. S'iṟappaṟiya oṟṟinkaṇ s'eyyaṟka; s'eyyin
puṟappaḍuttān ākum maṟai.

CHAPTER 59—ON SPIES

581. Verily the two eyes of a king are espionage and the celebrated code of laws.

582. A king's duty is to get day to day knowledge of everything that happens.

583. The sure way of achieving success for a king is to get correct information from spies.

584. Espionage consists of watching all people, to wit, the king's employees, his relations and his enemies.

585. An able spy puts on undoubted disguise, does not fear when detected, and never reveals his purpose.

586. A spy in the guise of an ascetic should gather information however difficult and should never be tired whatever be the troubles.

587. A spy should secure knowledge of things secret and should have no doubt about his information.

588. One must get confirmed the information supplied by one spy, by that of another.

589. Let the engagement of one spy be not known to another. Accept the information supplied independently by three spies.

590. Let not a king honour the spy publicly; for, by so doing he will be letting out his own secret.

CHAPTER 60—ŪKKAMUḌAIMAI

591. Uḍaiyar eṉappaḍuvadu ūkkam; ahdillār
uḍaiyatu uḍaiyarō maṟṟu.

592. Uḷḷam uḍaimai uḍaimai; poruḷuḍaimai
nillātu nīṅki viḍum.

593. Ākkam iḻandēm eṉṟuallāvār ūkkam
oruvantam kaittuḍai yār.

594. Ākkam atarviṉāyc cellum as'aivilā
ūkkam uḍaiyā ṉuḻai.

595. Veḷḷattu aṉaiya malarnīṭṭam; māndartam
uḷḷattu aṉaiyadu uyarvu.

596. Uḷḷuvadu ellām uyarvuuḷḷal; maṟṟatu
taḷḷiṉum taḷḷāmai nīrttu.

597. S'itaiviḍattu olkār uravōr; pudaiambiṉ
paṭṭuppāḍu ūṉṟun kaḷiṟu.

598. Uḷḷam ilātavar eytār ulakattu
vaḷḷiyam eṉṉum s'erukku.

599. Pariyatu kūrnkōṭṭatu āyiṉum yāṉai
verūum pulitāk kuṟiṉ.

600. Uramoruvaṟku uḷḷa veṟukkai; ahdillār
maram; makkaḷ ātalē vēṟu.

CHAPTER 60—ON EXERTION

591. One's real possession is one's exertion. If one does not have it, can one be said to really possess anything else ?

592. Exertion alone is one's wealth; inconstant material wealth will pass away.

593. Those who possess constant exertion will not grieve over the loss of their wealth.

594. Prosperity will discover a route to a person of undaunted will.

595. The length of a watery plant is determined by the depth of the water. Likewise the greatness of a person is proportionate to the strength of his will power.

596. In all acts and deeds, let exertion be one's ideal. Even if it were unattainable, its presence is enough.

597. The elephant stands undaunted despite piercing arrows ; so too, a person of strong will, will not get discouraged even in a losing concern.

598. A man of no strong will, cannot win the esteem of the world for his action.

599. Even the huge elephant with sharp tusks dreads the attacking tiger.

600. One's strength is one's exertion. Without it persons are only trees in the form of men.

CHAPTER 61—MAṬIYIN̲MAI

601. Kuḍiyen̲n̲um kun̲ṟā viḷakkam maṭiyen̲n̲um
māsūra māyntu keḍum.

602. Maṭiyai maṭiyā oḻukal kuḍiyaik
kuḍiyāka vēṇḍu pavar.

603. Maṭimaṭik koṇḍoḻukum pēdai piṟanda
kuḍimaṭiyum tan̲n̲in̲um mundu.

604. Kuḍimaṭindu kuṟṟam perukum maṭimaṭindu
māṇḍa uñaṟṟi lavarkku.

605. Neḍunīr maṟavi maṭituyil nāṉkum
keḍunīrār kāmak kalan̲.

606. Paḍiyuḍaiyār paṟṟamaintak kaṇṇum maṭiyuḍaiyār
māṇpayan̲ eytal aridu.

607. Iḍipurindu eḷḷumsol kēṭpar maṭipurindu
māṇḍa uñaṟṟui lavar.

608. Maṭimai kuḍimaikkaṇ tangin̲tan̲ on̲n̲ārkku
aḍimai pukutti viḍum.

609. Kudiāṇmai uḷvanda kuṟṟam oruvan̲
maṭiāṇmai māṟṟak keḍum.

610. Maṭiyilā man̲n̲avan̲ eytum aḍiyaḷandān̲
tāaya tellām orunku.

CHAPTER 61—AGAINST SLOTH

601. If sloth extends its darkness it will extinguish the lustrous lamp of one's family.

602. Those who wish the esteem of their family should never encourage sloth.

603. The family of the fool who hugs sloth in his own lap fades away before him.

604. Faults will be many among those who are devoid of exertion and will result in the ruin of their families.

605. Procrastination, carelessness, sluggardliness and sleep are the four boats fondly entered into by those who go to ruin.

606. Even when the wealth of the rulers of all earth is within his reach, the slothful will hardly derive any great benefit from it.

607. Lovers of idleness with no praiseworthy exertion will be the butt of disgrace and will receive words of rebuke.

608. If sloth comes to stay in one's family, it will make one the slave of one's enemies.

609. By conquering sloth, one can wipe out the reproach that has come over one's family.

610. All the universe once measured by the God will be with the king of no sloth.

CHAPTER 62—ĀḶVIṈAIYUḌAIMAI

611. Arumai uḍaitteṉṟu as'avāmai vēṇḍum:
perumai muyaṟci tarum.

612. Viṉaikkaṇ viṉaikeḍal ōmpal viṉaikkuṟai
tīrndāriṉ tīrndaṉṟu ulaku.

613. Tāḷāṇmai eṉṉum takaimaikkaṇ tankiṟṟē
vēḷāṇmai eṉṉum s'erukku.

614. Tāḷāṇmai illātāṉ vēḷāṇmai pēḍikai
vāḷāṇmai pōlak keḍum.

615. Iṉbam viḻaiyāṉ viṉaiviḻaivāṉ taṉkēḷir
tuṉban tuḍaittūṉṟum tūṇ.

616. Muyaṟci tiruviṉai yākkum: muyaṟṟiṉmai
iṉmai pukutti viḍum.

617. Maṭiyuḷāḷ māmukaṭi yeṉba: maṭiyilāṉ
tāḷuḷāḷ tāmaraiyi ṉāḷ.

618. Poṟiyiṉmai yārkkum paḻiyaṉṟu aṟivaṟindu
āḷviṉai iṉmai paḻi.

619. Deyvattāṉ ākādu eṉiṉum muyaṟcitaṉ
meyvaruttak kūli tarum.

620. Ūḻaiyum uppakkam kāṇpar ulaiviṉṟit
tāḻādu uñaṟṟu pavar.

CHAPTER 62—ON PERSEVERANCE

611. "Do not give up (your task) saying 'O' It is very difficult." The art of doing it comes of exertion.

612. Do not give up your task in the middle; for the world will abandon those who leave their task unfinished.

613. The greatness which consists in helping others dwells in the virtue of persevering effort.

614. The service of one with no persevering effort is vain like the sword wielded by a hermaphrodite.

615. One who does not seek pleasure but delights in work will be a pillar of support to one's relatives in their sorrow.

616. Exertion achieves wealth; absence of it brings on poverty.

617. Goddess of misfortune dwells in sloth; the Goddess of fortune lives in exertion.

618. Ill-luck is no disgrace; but it is a disgrace if one does not exert himself as to what should be done.

619. Though fate should ordain failure, bodily exertion will yield its own reward.

620. Those who labour hard, undaunted by obstacles will overcome destiny.

CHAPTER 63—IḌUKKAṈAḺIYĀMAI

621. Iḍukkaṉ varunkāl nakuka : ataṉai
aḍuttūrvadu ahdoppa dil.

622. Veḷḷat taṉaiya iḍumbai aṟivuḍaiyāṉ
uḷḷattiṉ uḷḷak keḍum.

623. Iḍumbaikku iḍumbai paḍuppar iḍumbaikku
iḍumbai paḍāa tavar.

624. Maḍuttavāy ellām pakaḍuaṉṉāṉ uṟṟa
iḍukkaṉ iḍarppāḍu uḍaittu.

625. Aḍukki variṉum aḻivilāṉ uṟṟa
iḍukkaṉ iḍukkaṉ paḍum.

626. Aṟṟēm eṉṟuallal paḍupavō peṟṟēmeṉṟu
ōmbutal tēṟṟā tavar.

627. Ilakkam uḍambu iḍumbaikku eṉṟu kalakkattaik
kaiyāṟāk koḷḷātām mēl.

628. Iṉbam viḻaiyāṉ iḍumbai iyalpeṉpāṉ
tuṉbam uṟutal ilaṉ.

629. Iṉbattuḷ iṉbam viḻaiyātāṉ tuṉbattuḷ
tuṉbam uṟutal ilaṉ.

630. Iṉṉāmai iṉbam eṉakkoḷiṉ ākuntaṉ
oṉṉār viḻaiyuñ ciṟappu.

END OF ARAS'IYAḶ

CHAPTER 63—ON COURAGE

621. Laugh over your obstacles; nothing like it to push them further and further.

622. Troubles like a flood will be overcome by a courageous thought rising in the minds of the wise.

623. The courageous will be causing sorrow to sorrow itself.

624. Just as the buffalo drags a cart through miry depth, one who fights on will overcome his difficulties.

625. The troubles of one who braves a series of adversity wear out and disappear.

626. Will those who do not during prosperity exultingly say "we are rich", cry out (during adversity) "Oh, we are destitute"?

627. The great know that the body is ever the target of trouble and will not regard trouble as trouble at all.

628. He who never gives way to sorrow, will not long for pleasure; he will regard trouble as quite natural.

629. He who does seek for pleasure in pleasure will not be vexed in sorrow.

630. One who regards trouble as pleasure will gain the elevation which his enemies desire (for themselves).

END OF KINGSHIP

ANGAVIYAL

CHAPTER 64—AMAICCU

631. Karuviyum kālamum s'eykaiyum s'eyyum
aruviṉaiyum māṇḍadu amaiccu.

632. Vaṉkaṇ kuḍikāttal kaṟṟaṟital āḷviṉaiyōḍu
ainduḍaṉ māṇḍadu amaiccu.

633. Pirittalum pēṇik koḷalum pirindārp
poruttalum valladu amaiccu.

634. Teritalum tērndu s'eyalum orutalaiyāc
collalum valladu amaiccu.

635. Aṟaṉaṟindu āṉṟamainda s'ollāṉeñ ñāṉṟum
tiṟaṉaṟindāṉ tērccit tuṇai.

636. Matinuṭpam nūlōḍuḍaiyārkku atinuṭpam
yāvuḷa muṉṉiṟ pavai.

637. S'eyaṟkai yaṟindak kaḍaittum ulakat
tiyaṟkai yaṟindu s'eyal.

638. Aṟikoṉṟu aṟiyāṉ eṉiṉum uṟuti
uḷaiyirundāṉ:kūṟal kaḍaṉ.

639. Paḻudeṇṇum mantiriyiṉ pakkattuḷ tevvōr
eḻupatu kōḍi uṟum.

640. Muṟaippaḍac cūḻntum muḍivilavē s'eyvar;
tiṟappāḍu ilā a tavar.

SECTION II. LIMBS OF THE STATE

CHAPTER 64—ON MINISTERS

631. He is the minister who finds out the means, the time, the deed and its full accomplishment.

632. A minister should have five qualities; tenacity of purpose, birth in a respectable family, welfare of the people, profound learning and perseverance.

633. A minister must be able to separate a foe from his ally, befriend allies and reunite separated allies.

634. A minister should study the consequences of an act and carry it successfully by a decisive speech.

635. He is a helpful counsellor who is righteous and considerate in his speech, and always knows how to act.

636. To a keen intellect combined with learning no difficulty stands in the way.

637. Even though you know the rules, act in conformity with the world opinion.

638. Though a king listens not to wise words it is the duty of the minister to speak firmly to him.

639. A treacherous minister by the king's side is equal to seventy crores of enemies.

640. Ministers who have no requisite ability will leave a task unfinished though well begun,

CHAPTER 65—S'OLVAṈMAI

641. Nānalam eṉṉum nalaṉ uḍaimai : annalam
yānalat tuḷḷaḍūum aṉṟu.

642. Ākkamum kēḍum adaṉāl varutalāl
kāttōmbal s'olliṉkaṇ s'ōrvu.

643. Kēṭṭārp piṇikkun takaiyavāyk kēḷārum
vēṭpa moḻivadāñ col.

644. Tiṟaṉaṟindu s'olluka s'ollai ; aṟaṉum
poruḷum adaṉiṉ ūnku il.

645. S'olluka s'ollaip piṟitōrs'ol accollai
vellums'ol iṉmai yaṟindu.

646. Vēṭpattām s'ollip piṟars'ol payaṉkōḍal
māṭciyiṉ mās'aṟṟār kōḷ.

647. S'olalvallaṉ s'ōrvilaṉ añjāṉ avaṉai
ikalvellal yārkkum aritu.

648. Viraindu toḻilkēṭkum ñālam nirantiṉitu
s'ollutal vallārp peṟiṉ.

649. Palas'ollak kāmuṟuvar maṉramā s'aṟṟa
s'ilas'ollal tēṟṟā tavar.

650. Iṇarūḻttum nāṟā malaraṉaiyar kaṟṟadu
uṇara viritturaiyā tār.

CHAPTER 65—ON GOOD SPEECH

641. The virtue of good speech is greater than all the other good qualities found in one.

642. As both prosperity and ruin are caused by words, a minister must guard against imperfection in his speech.

643. The minister must use such words as have the effect of strengthening the approval of those who agree and differ.

644. Speak having regard to one's capacity to listen; for there is no greater virtue nor wealth than that.

645. Speak out what you have to say only after knowing that your own argument will not be turned against you.

646. A good minister wins the approval of the listener by persuasive speech.

647. A clever speaker is neither tired nor fearful; none can defeat him in a debate.

648. Cogent reasoning and soft speech can bring the people over to one's side.

649. Those who cannot say a few words correctly will evince a desire to speak much.

650. Those who cannot explain well what they have learnt resemble the odourless flowers with their petals open.

CHAPTER 66—VIṈAITTŪYMAI

651. Tuṇainalam ākkam tarūum : viṉainalam
vēṇḍiya vellān tarum.

652. Eṉṟum oruvutal vēṇḍum pukaḷoḍu
naṉṟi payavā viṉai.

653. Ōotal vēṇḍum oḷimāḷkum s'eyviṉai
āadum eṉṉum avar.

654. Iḍukkaṇ paḍiṉum iḷivanda s'eyyār
naḍukkaṟṟa kāṭci yavar.

655. Eṟṟeṉ ṟuirankuva s'eyyaṟka : s'eyvāṉēṉ
maṟṟaṉṉa s'eyyāmai naṉṟu.

656. Īṉṟāl pas'i kāṇpāṉ āyiṉuṃ s'eyyaṟka
s'āṉṟōr paḻikkum viṉai.

657. Paḻimalain deydiya ākkattiṉ s'aṉṟōr
kaḻinal kuravē talai.

658. Kaḍinda kaḍindurār s'eydārkku avaitām
muḍindālum pīḻai tarum.

659. Aḻakkoṇḍa vellām aḻappōm : iḻappiṉum
piṟpayakkum naṟpā lavai.

660. Calattāṟ poruḷs'eydu ēmārttal pas'umaṇ
kalattuḷnīr peydirī i̤yaṟṟu.

CHAPTER 66—ON PURITY IN ACTION

651. A man's friends bring prosperity to him; but his good acts fetch him his wish.

652. That deed must always be discarded which does not promote virtue and produce fame.

653. Those who wish to become great must always avoid deeds which darken the lustre of their reputation.

654. Even adversity does not prompt men of unswerving purity to do mean things.

655. Desist from deeds which you may regret later; but if you once happen to do such a deed, repeat it not.

656. Though you find your mother starving, do not do anything which will be condemned by the great.

657. Better the poverty adopted by the great than the wealth resulting from sin.

658. Those who do knowingly forbidden things will suffer in the end, although they may succeed in doing them.

659. What is secured by causing tears to others will be lost with tears. But good deeds will result in good later.

660. A minister who promotes his king's resources by fraud is like one who tries to store up water in a pot of unburnt clay.

CHAPTER 67—VIṈAIT TIṬPAM

661. Viṉaittiṭpam eṉpadu oruvaṉ maṉattiṭpam
maṟṟaiya ellām piṟa.

662. Ūṟorāl uṟṟapiṉ olkāmai ivviraṇḍiṉ
āṟeṉpar āyndavar kōḷ.

663. Kaḍaikkoṭkac ceytakkatu āṇmai iḍaikkoṭkiṉ
eṟṟā viḻumam tarum.

664. S'ollutal yārkkum eḷitu: ariyavām
s'olliya vaṇṇañ ceyal.

665. Viṟeydi māṇḍār viṉaittiṭpam vēndaṉkaṇ
ūṟeydi uḷḷap paḍum.

666. Eṇṇiya eṇṇiyāṅku eytupa eṇṇiyār
tiṇṇiyar ākap peṟiṉ.

667. Uruvukaṇḍu eḷḷāmai vēṇḍum: uruḷperumtērkku
accāṇi aṉṉār uḍaittu.

668. Kalangādu kaṇḍa viṉaikkaṇ tuḷangādu
tūkkan kaḍindu s'eyal.

669. Tuṉbam uṟavariṉum s'eyka, tuṇivāṟṟi
iṉbam payakkum viṉai.

670. Eṉaittiṭpam eytiyak kaṇṇum viṉaittiṭpam
vēṇḍārai vēṇḍadu ulaku.

CHAPTER 67—ON RESOLUTENESS

661. Determination in action is one's resolution. All others are nothing.

662. Ministers versed in lore will not do unprofitable deeds, and if they do, they will not regret it.

663. A clever minister publishes a deed after its completion; if it becomes public in the intermediate stage, it will end in trouble.

664. It is easy for one to say, but it is difficult to do it in the said manner.

665. The resolution of a thoughtful and good minister in strengthening his monarch will earn all praise.

666. Firm of purpose, ministers carry out their resolution.

667. Do not despise one for lack of personality. Does not the little nail of the chariot keep the wheel going?

668. What you have clearly decided to do, do it without hesitation and delay.

669. Be resolute in deed which ends in happiness, though troublesome at the beginning.

670. The world will not esteem him who has no determined will, notwithstanding his other strong virtues.

CHAPTER 68—VIṈAIS'EYAL VAKAI

671. S'ūḻcci muḍivu tuṇiveytal attuṇivu
tāḻcciyuḷ tangutal tītu.

672. Tūnguka tūngic ceyaṟpāla: tūngaṟka
tūngātu s'eyyum viṉai.

673. Ollumvāy ellām viṉainaṉṟē: ollākkāl
s'ellumvāy nōkkic ceyal.

674. Viṉaipakai yeṉṟirandiṉ eccam niṉaiyunkāl
tīyeccam pōlat teṟum.

675. Poruḷkaruvi kālam viṉaiyiḍaṉoḍu aintum
iruḷtīra eṇṇic ceyal.

676. Muḍivum iḍaiyūṟum muṟṟiyāngu eydum
paḍupayaṉum pārttuc ceyal.

677. S'eyviṉai s'eyvāṉ s'eyalmuṟai avviṉai
uḷḷaṟivāṉ uḷḷan koḷal.

678. Viṉaiyāṉ viṉaiyākkik kōḍal naṉaikavuḷ
yāṉaiyāl yānaiyāt taṟṟu.

679. Naṭṭārkku nalla s'eyaliṉ viraintatē
oṭṭārai yoṭṭik koḷal.

680. Uṟais'iṟiyār uḷnaḍungal añjik kuṟaipeṟiṉ
koḷvar periyārp paṇindu.

CHAPTER 68—ON THE MEANS OF ACTION

671. Decision is the result of deliberation. It is harmful to rest it low.

672. Delay such things as call for delay. But never delay that which cannot be delayed.

673. Achieve a thing wherever possible; if it were not possible adopt a cautious policy.

674. An unfinished deed and an unfinished fight will like a half extinguished fire, cause ultimate harm.

675. Do a thing after carefully deliberating on five things: resources, means, the time, the nature of the deed, and the place.

676. In doing a thing, weigh deeply your aim, the hindrances and the final gain thereof.

677. The manner in which a thing should be done is to be determined after consulting an expert.

678. Use one act to achieve another just as one wild elephant is used to capture another.

679. It is much more urgent to secure the alliance of one's enemies, than to do good to one's friends.

680. Fearing that their weak king may quake with fear, ministers will bow before superior kings and accept their terms.

CHAPTER 69—TŪTU

681. Aṉpuḍaimai āṉṟa kuḍippiṟattal vēndavām
paṇpuḍaimai tūturaippāṉ paṇpu.

682. Aṉbaṟivu ārāynda s'olvaṉmai tūturaippārkku
iṉṟi yamaiyāta mūṉṟu.

683. Nūlāruḷ nūlvallaṉ ākutal vēlāruḷ
veṉṟi viṉaiyuraippāṉ paṇpu.

684. Aṟivuruvu ārāynta kalvi im mūṉṟaṉ
s'eṟivuḍaiyāṉ s'elka viṉaikku.

685. Tokac collit tūvāta nīkki nakaccolli
naṉṟı payappadān tūtu.

686. Kaṟṟukkaṇ añjāṉ s'elaccollik kālattāl
takkadu aṟivatām tūtu.

687. Kaḍaṉaṟindu kālam karudi iḍaṉaṟindu
eṇṇi uraippāṉ talai.

688. Tūymaı tuṇaimai tuṇivuḍaimai immūṉṟiṉ
vāymai vaḻiyurappāṉ paṇpu.

689. Viḍumāṟṟam vēndārkku uraippāṉ vaḍumāṟṟam
vāys'ōrā vaṉka ṇavaṉ.

690. Iṟuti payappiṉum eñjādu iṟaivaṟku
uṟuti payappadām tūtu.

CHAPTER 69—ON EMBASSY

681. The characteristics of an ambassador are loveability, noble birth and other qualities which evoke the monarch's respect.

682. Love, wisdom, ability to talk with full knowledge, are the three indispensable qualities of an ambassador.

683. A skilful ambassador who wishes to gain his mission among other monarchs wielding the spear must be more learned than the learned.

684. Only those who have wisdom, personality and mature scholarship must be sent on a mission.

685. A good ambassador is he who can talk cogently and sweetly and who is not offensive even in saying things that are disagreeable.

686. The envoy must be learned, fearless, persuasive and expedient.

687. The best envoy states his case convincingly knowing his duty at the proper time and place.

688. The qualifications of a true envoy are morality, loyalty to his monarch and courage.

689. He who does not falter even when faced with personal danger is fit to deliver his king's message.

690. A true envoy delivers his message even at the risk of death.

CHAPTER 70—MAṈṈARAIC CĒRNDOḶUKAL

691. Akalādu aṇukādu tīkkāyvār pōlka
ikalvēndarc cērndoḷuku vār.

692. Maṉṉar viḷaipa viḷaiyāmai maṉṉarāṉ
maṉṉiya ākkam tarum.

693. Pōṟṟiṉ ariyavai pōṟṟal: kaḍuttapiṉ
tēṟṟutal yārkkum aritu.

694. S'eviccollum s'ērnda nakaiyum avittoḷukal
āṉṟa periyār akattu.

695. Epporuḷum ōrār toḍarār maṟṟu apporuḷai
viṭṭakkāl kēṭka maṟai.

696. Kuṟippaṟindu kālan karudi veṟuppila
vēṇḍupa vēṭpac colal.

697. Vēṭpaṉa s'olli viṉaiyila eññāṉṟum
kēṭpiṉuñ collā viḍal.

698. Iḷaiyar iṉamuṟaiyar eṉṟikaḷār niṉṟa
oḷiyōḍu oḷukap paḍum.

699. Koḷappaṭṭēm eṉṟeṉṉik koḷḷāta s'eyyār
tuḷakkaṟṟa kāṭci yavar.

700. Paḷaiyam eṉakkarudip paṇpalla s'eyyum
keḷutakaimai kēḍu tarum.

CHAPTER 70—ON CO-OPERATION WITH KING

691. Those who personally serve the monarch do not go too near him or too far away from him, like those who warm themselves by the fire side.

692. Not to covet those things which are desired by the monarch produce lasting wealth.

693. To save himself a minister must avoid gross faults, for it is difficult to please, once being found fault with.

694. In the presence of the great avoid whispering and smiling.

695. Let not the minister lend ear to the king's secret or be inquisitive to know it. But let him listen to it when the king reveals it.

696. Watch the mood of the monarch. Talk to him pleasantly and inoffensively.

697. Speak desirable things though unasked, but abstain from profitless talk although solicited by him.

698. Do not disrespect a king on the ground of age or kinship, but behave as befits his royalty.

699. Men of high intelligence, respected by a king will not indulge in things revolting to him.

700. To take liberty under the cover of old acquaintance and do unwanted things is to court ill,

CHAPTER 71—KUṞIPPAṞITAL

701. Kūṟāmai nōkkik kuṟippaṟivāṉ eññāṉṟum
māṟāṉīr vaiyakku aṇi.

702. Aiyap paḍā adu akattatu uṇarvāṉait
deyvattōḍu oppak koḷal.

703. Kuṟippiṉ kuṟippuṇar vārai uṟuppiṉuḷ
yādu koḍuttum koḷal.

704. Kuṟittadu kūṟāmaik koḷvārōḍu ēṉai
uṟuppōr aṉaiyarāl vēṟu.

705. Kuṟippiṉ kuṟippuṇarā vāyiṉ uṟuppiṉuḷ
eṉṉa payattavō kaṇ.

706. Aḍuttatu kāṭṭum paḷingupōl neñjam
kaḍuttatu kāṭṭum mukam.

707. Mukattiṉ mudukkuṟaindadu uṇḍō uvappiṉum
kāyiṉun tāṉmun tuṟum.

708. Mukanōkki niṟka amaiyum akanōkki
uṟṟadu uṇarvārp peṟin.

709. Pakaimaiyum kēṇmaiyum kaṇṇuraikkum kaṇṇiṉ
vakaimai yuṇarvārp peṟiṉ.

710. Nuṇṇiyam eṉpār aḷakkunkōl kāṇunkāḷ
kaṇṇallatu illai piṟa.

CHAPTER 71—ON READING ONE'S INTENTIONS

701. He who is able to divine one's hidden intentions is a jewel among men on this sea-girt earth.

702. He who would speak out fearlessly what he feels will be regarded equal to God.

703. The king at any cost should secure among his associates one who can discover by intuition another's unexpressed thoughts.

704. Those who are able to discover unexpressed thoughts may be deemed superior to other's service.

705. *Of what avail is the eye, among the organs of sense, if it does not note another's intentions?*

706. Like a mirror that reflects what is near it, the face will show what passes in the mind.

707. Is there anything more expressive than the face which is an index as well as agony?

708. If you come across one, who can read your face, study one's face as one does yours.

709. The eye proclaims friendliness and hostility to one who can read the message of the eyes.

710. There is no other measuring rod, used by intelligent ministers than the monarch's eye.

CHAPTER 72—AVAIYAṞITAL

711. Avaiyaṟin dārāyndu s'olluka: s'olliṉ
tokaiyaṟinda tūymai yavari.

712. Iḍaiteṟindu nankuṇarndu s'olluka s'olliṉ
naḍaiterinda naṉmai yavar.

713. Avaiyaṟiyār s'ollalmēṟ koḷpavar s'olliṉ
vakaiyaṟiyār: vallatūm il.

714. Oḷiyārmuṉ oḷḷiyar ātal: veḷīyārmuṉ
vāṉs'utai vaṇṇan koḷal.

715. Naṉṟeṉṟa vaṟṟuḷḷum naṉṟē muduvaruḷ
mundu kiḷavāc ceṟivu.

716. Āṟṟiṉ nilaitaḷarn daṟṟē viyaṉpulam
ēṟṟuṇarvār muṉṉar iḻukku.

717. Kaṟṟaṟindār kalvi viḷangum kas'aḍaṟac
coṟṟerital vallār akattu.

718. Uṇarva duḍaiyārmuṉ s'ollal vaḷarvataṉ
pāttiyuḷ nīrs'orin daṟṟu.

719. Pullavaiyuḷ poccāntum s'ollaṟka nallavaiyuḷ
naṉku s'elaccollu vār.

720. Ankaṇattuḷ ukka amiḻtaṟṟāl tamkaṇattar
ḷallārmuṉ kōṭṭi koḷal.

CHAPTER 72—ON KNOWING THE ASSEMBLY

711. Men should weigh their words in speaking when addressing an audience.

712. Good people who know the value of the language they employ, must speak noting how their words are received.

713. The learning of those who speak without taking into consideration the assembly addressed or ignorant of the art of speaking can be of no use to them.

714. Before brilliant people be brilliant; before plain people be as plain as white chalk.

715. The humility to maintain silence before superiors is the best of all good qualities.

716. To be censured by an assembly of the learned wise is like losing one's balance while on the road to salvation.

717. The scholarship of the learned shines brilliantly before those who can appreciate faultless speech.

718. Speaking before the wise is like feeding crops with water.

719. Those who say good things before a good assembly should not even in forgetfulness say the same before the illiterate.

720. Entering an assembly of men of unequal respectability will be like pouring nectar in an unclean courtyard.

CHAPTER 73—AVAIYAÑJĀMAI

721. Vakaiyaṟindu vallavai vāys'ōrār s'olliṉ
tokaiyaṟinda tūymai yavar.

722. Kaṟṟāruḷ kaṟṟār eṉappaḍuvar kaṟṟārmuṉ
kaṟṟa s'elaccollu vār.

723. Pakaiyakattuc cāvār eḷiyar: ariyar
avaiyakattu añjā tavar.

724. Kaṟṟārmuṉ kaṟṟa s'elaccollit tānkaṟṟa
mikkāruḷ mikka koḷal.

725. Āṟṟiṉ aḷavaṟindu kaṟka: avaiyañjā
māṟṟam koḍuttaṟ poruṭṭu.

726. Vāloḍeṉ vaṉkaṇṇar allārkku nūloḍeṉ
nuṇṇavai añju pavarkku.

727. Pakaiyakattup pēḍikai oḷvāḷ avaiyakattu
añjumavaṉ kaṟṟa nūl.

728. Pallavai kaṟṟum payamilarē nallavaiyuḷ
naṉku s'elaccollā tār.

729. Kallāta variṉ kaḍaiyeṉba kaṟṟaṟindu
nallār avaiyañju vār.

730. Ulareṉinum illāroḍu oppar kaḷaṉañjik
kaṟṟa s'elaccollā tāṟ.

CHAPTER 73—NOT TO BE AFRAID OF ASSEMBLY

721. The expert in the art of speaking will not flounder, addressing an assembly of the learned.

722. Those will be deemed foremost among the learned, who can speak learned things acceptable to the learned.

723. Many die in the field of battle. But few are those who can fear fools addressing an assembly.

724. Speak to the learned what you have learnt, and receive from them much that you have to learn.

725. Understand the full scope of learning and learn, so that you may, without fear, reply effectively in an assembly.

726. Of what use is the sword for the unvaliant? Likewise of what use is learning for the timid to face an assembly?

727. The learning of one afraid of an assembly is like the shining sword in the hands of an eunuch in a battle-field.

728. Vain is the versed learning of one who cannot address with profit a learned assembly.

729. The learned who are afraid of a good assembly will be regarded as worse than the illiterate.

730. Dead though alive are those who are afraid to address an assembly on what they have learnt.

CHAPTER 74—NĀḌU

731. Taḷḷā viḷaiyuḷum takkārum tāḷvilāc
celvarum s'ērvaṭu nāḍu.

732. Perumporuḷāl peṭṭakka tāki arunkēṭṭāl
āṟṟa viḷaivadu nāḍu.

733. Poṟaiyorungu mēlvarunkāl tāngi iṟaivaṟku
iṟaiyorungu nērvatu nāḍu.

734. Uṟupas'iyum ōvāp piṇiyum s'eṟupakaiyum
s'ērā diyalvadu nāḍu.

735. Palkuḻuvum pāḻs'eyyum uṭpakaiyum vēndalaikkum
kolkuṟumbum illatu nāḍu.

736. Kēḍaṟiyāk keṭṭa iḍattum vaḷankuṉṟā
nāḍeṉpa nāṭṭiṉ talai.

737. Irupuṉalum vāynda malaiyum varupuṉalum
vallaraṇum nāṭṭiṟku uṟuppu.

738. Piṇiyiṉmai s'elvam viḷaivuiṉbam ēmam
aṇiyeṉba nāṭṭiṟkuiv vaindu.

739. Nāḍeṉba nāḍā vaḷattaṉa: nāḍalla
nāḍa vaḷantaru nāḍu.

740. Ānkamai veytiyak kaṇṇum payamiṉṟē
vēndamai illāta nāḍu.

CHAPTER 74—ON THE KINGDOM

731. That is a kingdom which has undiminishing produce, righteous people and fadeless riches.

732. That is a kingdom which has boundless wealth coveted for by other nations and has imperishable fertile resources.

733. That alone is a kingdom which accommodates immigrants and whose king receives taxes willingly paid.

734. That is a kingdom where excessive hunger, incurable diseases and destructive enemies are absent.

735. That is a kingdom where there are not many (disloyal) associations, destructive internal dissensions and disturbing murderous chieftains.

736. That is the top kingdom which is not harassed by an enemy, and which even if harassed does not experience want.

737. Surface and subsoil water, well situated hills from which flow waters and an invincible fort are the limbs of a kingdom.

738. Five are the ornaments of a kingdom—absence of disease, wealth, fertility, happiness and security.

739. That is a kingdom which has rich natural resources. That is no kingdom which yields wealth by toil.

740. Vain is the kingdom which may have all the excellence except harmony between the ruler and the ruled.

CHAPTER 75—ARAṆ

741. Āṟṟu pavarkkum araṇporuḷ añjittaṉ
pōṟṟu pavarkkum poruḷ.

742. Maṇinīrum maṇṇum malaiyum aṇiniḻal
kāḍum uḍaiyadu araṇ.

743. Uyarvu akalam tiṇmai arumaiin nāṉkiṉ
amaivaraṇ eṉṟuraikkum nūl.

744. S'iṟukāppiṉ pēriḍatta tāki uṟupakai-
ūkkam aḻippadu araṇ.

745. Koḷaṟkaritāyk koṇḍakūḻt tāki akattār
nilaikku eḷitām nīradu araṇ.

746. Ellāp poruḷum uḍaittāy iḍattutavum
nalāḷ uḍaiyadu araṇ.

747. Muṟṟiyum muṟṟādu eṟindum aṟaippaḍuttum
paṟṟaṟku ariyadu araṇ.

748. Muṟṟāṟṟi muṟṟi yavaraiyum paṟṟāṟṟip
paṟṟiyār velvadu araṇ.

749. Muṉaimukattu māṟṟalar s'āya viṉaimukattu
vīṟeydi māṇḍadu araṇ.

750. Eṉaimāṭcıt tākiyak kaṇṇum viṉaimāṭci
illārkaṇ illadu araṇ.

CHAPTER 75—ON FORTRESS

741. A fortress is important alike to a conquering foe and a timid defender.

742. It is a fortress which has sparkling water, open spaces, hills and cool and shady forests round.

743. Treatises on fortification state that the walls of a stronghold should be lofty, broad, strong and inaccessible.

744. A fortress which has a name as a natural defence cools the heat of the attacking foe.

745. A good fortress is that which is inaccessible, is sufficiently provided and is easily defensible from within.

746. A fortress shall have all things needed by its residents including capable warriors.

747. A good fortress cannot be besieged or taken by storm or be undermined.

748. The inmates of a good fortress can defend themselves even when besieged on all sides.

749. That fortress is famous which makes it possible for its defenders to destroy the besiegers even at the outset.

750. Of what use are these barriers of defence to a stronghold if it possesses no men of valour.

CHAPTER 76—PORUḶ S'EYAL VAKAI

751. Poruḷal lavaraip poruḷākac ceyyum
poruḷalladu illai poruḷ.

752. Illārai ellārum eḷḷuvar ; s'elvarai
yellārum s'eyvar s'iṛappu.

753. Poruḷeṉṉum poyyā viḷakkam iruḷaṛukkum
eṇṇiya tēyattuc ceṉṛu.

754. Aṛaṉīṉum iṉbamum īṉum tiṛaṉaṛindu
tītiṉṛi vanda poruḷ.

755. *Aruḷoḍum aṉboḍum vārāp poruḷākkam*
pullār puraḷa viḍal.

756. Uṛuporuḷum ulku poruḷuntaṉ oṉṉārt
teṛuporuḷum vēndaṉ poruḷ.

757. Aruḷeṉṉum aṉbīṉ kuḷavi poruḷeṉṉum
s'elvac ceviliyāl uṇḍu.

758. Kuṉṛēṛi yāṉaippōr kaṇḍaṛṛāl taṉkaittoṉṛu
uṇḍākac ceyvāṉ viṉai.

759. S'eyka poruḷaic : ceṛunar s'erukkaṛukkum
ehku adaṉiṉ kūrıya dil.

760. Oṇporuḷ kālppa iyaṛṛiyārkku eṉporuḷ
ēṉai iraṇḍum orunku.

CHAPTER 76—ON ACQUISITION OF WEALTH

751. There is nothing else than riches that make insignificant men prominent.

752. All will despise the poor; all will accord honour to the wealthy.

753. The faultless lamp of riches will dispel the darkness (of trouble) in any country to which it is taken.

754. The wealth accumulated justly and without sin will confer virtue and happiness.

755. Let not the king accept the wealth not acquired through mercy and love.

756. Unclaimed wealth, tolls and tributes by the subdued chieftains are the king's property.

757. What is mercy, but the child of love? What is wealth, but the nurse of mercy?

758. The deeds of the wealthy are like elephant fights witnessed from a hill.

759. Store up wealth; no other weapon is sharper than that to destroy the enemy's pride.

760. Amass wealth by lawful means; the other two (virtue and happiness) will follow.

CHAPTER 77—PAḌAI MĀṬCI

761. Uṛuppamaindu ūṛuañja velpaḍai vēndaṉ
veṛukkaiyuḷ ellān talai.

762. Ulaiviḍattu ūṛuañjā vaṉkaṇ tolaiviḍattut
tolpaḍaikku allāl aritu.

763. Olittakkāl eṉṉām uvari elippakai
nākam uyirppak keḍum.

764. Aḻiviṉṛu aṛaipōkā tāki vaḻivanda
vaṉkaṇ aduvē paḍai.

765. Kūṛṛuḍaṉṛu mēlvariṉum kūḍi etirniṛkum
āṛṛal aduvē paḍai.

766. Maṛammāṉam māṇḍa vaḻiccelavu tēṛṛam
eṉanāṉkē ēmam paḍaikku.

767. Tārtāngic celvatu tāṉai: talaivanda
pōrtāngun taṉmai aṇindu.

768. Aḍaltakaiyum āṛṛalum illeṉiṉum tāṉai
paḍaittakaiyāl pāḍu peṛum.

769. S'irumaiyum s'ellāt tuṉiyum vaṛumaiyum
illāyiṉ vellum paḍai.

770. Nilaimakkaḷ s'āla uḍaitteṉiṉum tāṉai
talaimakkaḷ ilvaḻi il.

CHAPTER 77—ON THE VALUE OF AN ARMY

761. A well-equipped and fearlessly conquering army is the foremost wealth of a king.

762. The heroic valour of rallying round the king even in adversity is peculiar to hereditary force, and not to others.

763. The hiss of a cobra stills for ever an army of rats as vast as the ocean.

764. It is a heroic force that is hereditary, undiminished in powers and not undermined by the enemy.

765. A valiant army faces courageously the advancing foe even when led by the God of Death.

766. Heroism, honour, tried policy and fidelity to the king, these four are an army's shelter.

767. That alone is an army which understands the enemy's tactics, and fearlessly advances.

768. An army by mere show can achieve distinction though it may lack bold advance or even self-protection.

769. It is a winning army which has neither littleness, nor irremoveable bitterness and poverty.

770. Of what avail is the army of heroic warriors if there be no general to guide them ?

CHAPTER 78—PAḌAIC CERUKKU

771. Eṉaimuṉ nillaṉmiṉ tevvir! palareṉai
muṉṉiṉṟu kalniṉ ṟavar.

772. Kāṉa muyaleyta ambiṉil yāṉai
piḻaitta vēl ēndal iṉitu.

773. Pērāṇmai eṉpa taṟukaṇ: oṉ ṟuṟṟakkāl
ūrāṇmai maṟṟataṉ ehku.

774. Kaivēl kaliṟṟoḍu pōkki varupavaṉ
meyvēl paṟiyā nakum.

775. Viḻittakaṇ vēlkoṇ ḍeṟiya aḻittu imaippiṉ
ōṭṭaṉṟō vaṉkaṇa varkku.

776. Viḻuppuṇ paḍātanāḷ ellām vaḻukkiṉuḷ
vaikkuntaṉ nāḷai yeḍuttu.

777. S'uḻalum is'aivēṇḍi vēṇḍā uyirār
kaḻalyāppuk kārikai nīrttu.

778. Uṟiṉuyir añjā maṟavar iṟaivaṉ
s'eṟiṉuñcīr kuṉṟal ilar.

779. Iḻaitta dikavāmaic cāvārai yārē
piḻaitta doṟukkiṟ pavar.

780. Purandārkaṇ nīrmalkac cākaṟpiṉ s'ākkāḍu
irandukōḷ takka duḍaittu.

CHAPTER 78—ON COURAGE OF THE ARMY

771. O, Enemies! Do not stand in front of our Lord; for many who stood before him are now standing as hero-stones.

772. Better to bear the spear hurled against an elephant, though it misses its aim, than the arrow aimed against a hare in the forest.

773. Fearlessness is a manly virtue; but in distress, mercy is its keen edge.

774. The warrior who hurls his spear against an advancing elephant enjoys to pull it from his body.

775. If the fierce look (of a warrior) winks at a dart aimed at him, it is tantamount to a retreat.

776. Reflecting on the days past, a hero regards those days vain in which he has not received a wound.

777. The anklet is a fitting adornment to warriors who fight fearless of life for a world-wide reputation.

778. Warriors unmindful of their lives in battle will not be daunted even by the wrath of their obstructing monarch.

779. Who can find fault with those (soldiers) who will lay down their lives to fulfil their vow?

780. Ye! Soldiers, endeavour to earn a death of glory which will move your chief to tears.

CHAPTER 79—NAṬPU

781. S'eyaṟkariya yāvuḷa naṭpiṉ: atupōl
viṉaikkariya yāvuḷa kāppu.

782. Niṟainīra nīravar kēṇmai piṟaimatip
piṉnīra pēdaiyār naṭpu.

783. Naviltoṟum nūlnayam pōlum payiltoṟum
paṇbuḍai yāḷar toḍarpu.

784. Nakutaṟ poruṭṭaṉṟu naṭṭal: mikutikkaṇ
mēṟceṉ ṟiḍittaṟ poruṭṭu.

785. Puṇarcci paḻakutal vēṇḍā: uṇarccitāṉ
naṭpān kiḻamai tarum.

786. Mukanaka naṭpatu naṭpaṉṟu; neñjattu
akanaka naṭpatu naṭpu.

787. Aḻiviṉ avainīkki āṟuuyttu aḻiviṉkaṇ
allal uḻappatām naṭpu.

788. Uḍukkai iḻandavaṉ kaipōla āṅkē
iḍukkaṇ kaḷaivatām naṭpu.

789. Naṭpiṟku vīṟṟirukkai yāteṉil koṭpu iṉṟi
ollumvāy ūṉṟum nilai.

790. Iṉaiyar ivaremakku iṉṉamyām eṉṟu
puṉaiyiṉum pulleṉṉum naṭpu.

CHAPTER 79—ON FRIENDSHIP

781. What is there more important than an ally; and what is more helpful than securing his aid.

782. The friendship of the wise resembles the waxing crescent; the friendship of the unwise fades away like the waning moon.

783. Even as good literature enraptures its reader the attachment of good men increases a king's happiness.

784. Friendship is made not for pleasure but it is a corrective to him who errs on the other side.

785. Friendship is not cultivated by mere acquaintance. It is the harmony that cements the bond of friendship.

786. Smile is no index for friendship. Real friendship makes the heart also smile.

787. Friendship prevents harmful deeds being committed and does beneficial things sharing the other's misfortunes.

788. Friendship removes suffering even as promptly as the hand which clutches the slipping garment.

789. If one asks where friendship abides, it lies in timely aid.

790. Even one may say, "These are my friends; I am deeply attached to them". Yet, it may be insignificant friendship.

CHAPTER 80—NAṬPĀRĀYTAL

791. Nāḍātu naṭṭaliṟ kēḍillai ; naṭṭapiṉ
vīḍillai naṭpāḷ pavarkku.

792. Āyndāyndu koḷḷātāṉ kēṇmai kaḍaimuṟai
tāṉs'āṉ tuyaram tarum.

793. Guṇaṉum kuḍimaiyum kuṟṟamum kuṉṟā
iṉaṉum aṟindu yākka naṭpu.

794. Kuḍippiṟandu taṉkaṇ paḻināṇu vāṉaik
koḍuttum koḷal vēṇḍum naṭpu.

795. Aḻaccolli alladu iḍittu vaḻakkaṟiya
vallārnaṭpu āyndu koḷal.

796. Kēṭṭiṉum uṇḍōr uṟuti ; kiḻaiñarai
nīṭṭi yaḷappadōr kōl.

797. Ūdiyam eṉpadu oruvaṟkup pēdaiyār
kēṇmai orīi viḍal.

798. Uḷḷaṟka uḷḷam s'iṟukuva : koḷḷaṟka
allaṟkaṇ āṟṟaṟuppār naṭpu.

799. Keḍunkālaik kaiviḍuvār kēṇmai aḍunkālai
uḷḷiṉum uḷḷañ cuḍum.

800. Maruvuka mās'aṟṟār kēṇmai ; oṉṟu ittum
oruvuka oppilār naṭpu.

CHAPTER 80—ON TRUE FRIENDSHIP

791. Nothing causes greater harm than the indiscriminate choice of friends; for one cannot give up one's chosen friends.

792. The friendship entered into without repeated tests causes grief till the end of one's life.

793. Make friends with one after knowing one's character, ancestry, defects and one's great associates.

794. Even by paying a price secure the friendship of one of noble family who fears a blot on his character.

795. Make after proper test friendship with the wise who make you weep for a crime and chastise when you err.

796. Adversity has its uses, for it is the touchstone that tries the genuine friend.

797. One must regard it as a windfall if one is able to shake off unwise friends.

798. Refrain from doing things which make your heart shrink. Likewise avoid friends who desert you in adversity.

799. Friendship of those who fall off in adversity continues to rankle in your heart of hearts till your death.

800. Count the friendship of the faultless and release yourself even at a price from friends not of approved conduct.

CHAPTER 81—PALAMAI

801. Palamai yenappaduvadu yādenin yādum
kilamaiyaik kīlndidā natpu.

802. Natpirku uruppuk kelutakaimai; marratarku
uppuātal s'ānrōr kadan.

803. Palakiya natpevan s'eyyum kelutakaimai
s'eytānku amaiyāk kadai.

804. Vilaitagaiyān vēndi yiruppar kelutakaiyāl
kēlātu nattār s'eyin.

805. Pēdaimai onrō perunkilamai enrunarka
nōtakka nattār s'eyin.

806. Ellaikkan ninrār turavār tolaividattum
tollaikkan ninrār todarpu.

807. Alivanda s'eyyinum anbuarār anbin
valivanda kēnmai yavar.

808. Kēlilukkam kēlāk kelutakaimai vallārkku
nālilukkam nāttar s'eyin.

809. Kedāa valivanda kēnmaiyār kēnmai
vidāar vilaiyum ulaku.

810. Vilaiyār vilaiyap padupa palaiyārkan
panbin talaippiriyā tār,

CHAPTER 81—ON OLD FRIENDSHIP

801. What is old friendship? It is that which willingly submits to friendly interferences.

802. The soul of friendship is perfect freedom. To be of cheer in friendly interference is the duty of the wise.

803. What use is old friendship if one's intimacy does not approve of one's acts?

804. If friends voluntarily do their duty through intimacy the wise accept it with approval.

805. If a friend acts contrary to one's wishes, treat it as not due to ignorance but to intimacy.

806. Old friends may do harm but it is the quality of friendship not to abandon them.

807. Old and loving friends, even when betrayed do not break off in their love.

808. Intimacy is the refusal to hear about friend's faults. Noble friends smile that day when their friends commit faults.

809. The world applauds long established friends who do not forsake one another.

810. Even foes long for those who do not forsake their old and erring friends.

CHAPTER 82—TĪNAṬPU

811. Parukuvār pōliṉum paṇbilār kēṇmai
perukaliṉ kuṉṟal iṉitu.

812. Uṟiṉnaṭṭu aṟiṉorūum oppilār kēṇmai
peṟiṉum iḻappiṉum eṉ.

813. Uṟuvatu s'īrtūkkum naṭpum peṟuvatu
koḷvārum kaḷvarum nēr.

814. Amarakattu āṟṟaṟukkum kallāmā aṉṉār
tamariṉ taṉimai talai.

815. S'eyduēmañ cārāc ciṟiyavar puṉkēṇmai
eytaliṉ eytāmai naṉṟu.

816. Pēdai perunkeḻīi naṭpiṉ aṟivuḍaiyār
ēdiṉmai kōḍi uṟum.

817. Nakaivakaiyar ākiya naṭpiṉ pakaivarāl
pattaḍutta kōḍi uṟum.

818. Ollum karumam uḍaṟṟupavar kēṇmai
s'ollāḍār s'ōra viḍal.

819. Kaṉaviṉum iṉṉātu maṉṉō viṉaivēṟu
s'olvēṟu paṭṭār toḍarpu.

820. Eṉaittum kuṟukutal ōmpal maṉaikkeḻīi
maṉṟil paḻippār toḍarpu.

CHAPTER 82—ON BASE ALLIANCE

811. Let that kind of friendship diminish rather than increase if it is really pretentious and devoid of genuine feeling.

812. What does it matter whether we gain or lose the equal friendship of those who befriend if advantageous to them and betray if disadvantageous ?

813. Those who value friendship for the gain thereof are only avaricious prostitutes and thieves.

814. Better solitude than the alliance of the wicked who fail like the unbroken steed its rider in the battlefield.

815. Better to abandon than contract the friendship of the lowly who do not aid you in adversity.

816. Very much more valuable is the hatred of the wise than the doting friendship of fools.

817. Ten thousand times better is the enmity of foes than the friendship which makes one a laughing stock.

818. Abandon without fuss friends who make a possible thing impossible.

819. The alliances of men whose words are different from their deeds afford no pleasure even in a dream.

820. Avoid the friendship however little, of those who befriend you at home but betray you in the assembly (public).

CHAPTER 83—KŪDĀNAṬPU

821. S'iriḍan kāṇiṉ eṟitaṟkup paṭṭaḍai
nērā nirantavar naṭpu.

822. Iṉampōṉṟu iṉamallār kēṇmai makaḷir
maṉampōla vēṟu paḍum.

823. Palanalla kaṟṟak kaḍaittum maṉamnallar
ākutal māṇārkku aritu.

824. Mukattiṉ iṉiya nakāa akattiṉṉā
vañjarai añjap paḍum.

825. Maṉattiṉ amaiyā tavarai eṉaittoṉṟum
s'olliṉāl tēṟaṟpāṟṟu aṉṟu.

826. Naṭṭārpōl nallavai s'olliṉum oṭṭārs'ol
ollai yuṇarap paḍum.

827. S'olvaṇakkam oṉṉārkaṇ koḷḷaṟka vilvaṇakkam
tīnku kuṟittamai yāṉ.

828. Toḻutakai yuḷḷum paḍaiyoḍungum; oṉṉār
aḻudakaṇ ṇīrum aṉaittu.

829. Mikacceydu tameḷ ḷuvārai nakacceydu
naṭpiṉuḷ s'āppullaṟ pāṟṟu.

830. Pakainaṭpu āmkālam varunkāl mukam naṭṭu
akanaṭpu orīi viḍal.

CHAPTER 83—ON FALSE ALLIANCE

821. Friendship of the wicked is but a pretext to stab you cunningly in an unwary mood.

822. Inconstant as the heart of a woman is the false friendship of seeming friends.

823. A wicked heart never mellows with learning.

824. Fear those who smile and smile but are villainy at heart.

825. It is impossible to convince those whose minds do not agree.

826. Of what avail are the friendly words of your foe ?

827. Do not trust the seeming humility of the enemy's speech for the bow bends only to do harm.

828. The folded hands of the enemy in an attitude of devotion, conceal a weapon. Likewise are his false tears.

829. Policy requires that hostility to a foe should be hidden under a smile.

830. When the enemy pretends alliance, receive him with outward smile and inward distrust.

CHAPTER 84—PĒDAIMAI

831. Pēdaimai eṉbadoṉṟu yādeṉiṉ ēdankoṇḍu
ūdiyam pōka viḍal.

832. Pēdaimai yuḷellām pēdaimai kādaṉmai
kaialla taṉkaṇ s'eyal.

833. Nāṇāmai nāḍāmai nāriṉmai yādoṉṟum
pēṇāmai pēdai toḻil.

834. Ōdi uṇarndum piṟarkku uraittum tāṉaḍankāp
pēdaiyiṉ pēdaiyār il.

835. Orumaic ceyalāṟṟum pēdai eḻumaiyum
tāṉpukku aḻundum aḷaṟu.

836. Poypaḍum oṉṟō puṉaipūṇum kaiyaṟiyāp
pēdai viṉaimēṟ koḷiṉ.

837. Ētilār ārat tamaṟpas'ippar, pēdai
peruñcelvam uṟṟak kaḍai.

838. Maiyal oruvaṉ kaḷittuaṟṟāl pēdaitaṉ
kaiyoṉṟu uḍaimai peṟiṉ.

839. Peritiṉidu pēdaiyār kēṇmai; pirivinkaṇ
pīḻai taruvatoṉṟu il.

840. Kaḻāakkāl paḷḷiyuḷ vaittaṟṟāl, s'āṉṟōr
kuḻāattup pēdai pukal.

CHAPTER 84—ON STUPIDITY

831. Stupidity clings to the evil and lets slip the good.

832. The crown of stupidity is the desire to do evil.

833. Shamelessness, negligence, arrogance and giddiness mark the stupid.

834. Most stupid is the learned fool who remains disloyal to his own noble teaching.

835. Acts of folly done in one birth cause misery to him in seven more births to come.

836. The task undertaken by a foolish man is spoiled and also ruined.

837. Strangers and not relatives fatten on the unlimited wealth of a fool.

838. A fool that lives by a fortune is like a mad man in his drunken glee.

839. Verily sweet are the uses of fools' love. For nothing is lost in a separation.

840. A fool's entry into the assembly of the wise is like one's unclean foot on the bed.

CHAPTER 85—PULLAṞIVĀṈMAI

841. Aṟiviṉmai iṉmaiyuḷ iṉmai : piṟitiṉmai
iṉmaiyā vaiyādu ulaku.

842. Aṟivilāṉ neñju uvandu ītal piṟitiyādum
illai : peṟuvān tavam.

843. Aṟivilār tāmtammaip pīḻikkum pīḻai
s'eṟuvārkkuñ ceytal aṟitu.

844. Veṇmai yeṉappaḍuvadu yādeṉiṉ oṇmai
uḍaiyamyām eṉṉum s'erukku.

845. Kallāda mēṟkoṇ ḍoḻukal kas'aḍaṟa
valladūum aiyan tarum.

846. Aṟṟam maṟaitalō pullaṟivu tamvayiṉ
kuṟṟam maṟaiyā vaḻi.

847. Arumaṟai s'ōrum aṟivilāṉ s'eyyum
perumiṟai tāṉē taṉakku.

848. Ēvavum s'eykalāṉ tāṉteṟāṉ : avvuyir
pōom aḷavumōr nōy.

849. Kāṇātāṉ kāṭṭuvān tāṉkāṇāṉ : kāṇātāṉ
kaṇḍāṉām tāṉkaṇḍa āṟu.

850. Ulakattār uṇḍeṉpadu illeṉpāṉ vaiyattu
alakaiyā vaikkap paḍum.

CHAPTER 85—ON IGNORANCE

841. Of all forms of poverty, poverty of intellect is the most serious; other forms of poverty are not regarded serious by the world.

842. If a fool makes a gift with pleasure, it is due to the recipient's luck.

843. The unwise inflict upon themselves more harm than the enemies can think of.

844. Where does conceit dwell but in the immature mind?

845. Pretension to knowledge beyond one's province makes men suspect the proficiency in one's own province.

846. What availeth one's garment if one's defects lie naked to the world?

847. A learned fool doth harm to himself.

848. A fool neither listens to wise counsel nor exerts himself. He will be a plague to the world till his death.

849. He who seeks to enlighten a fool befools himself. For the conceited fool thinks that he knows everything.

850. He who is out of tune with the world is regarded a demon.

CHAPTER 86—IKAL

851. Ikaleṉba, ellā uyirkkum pakaleṉṉum
paṇpiṉmai pārikkum nōy.

852. Pakalkarutip paṟṟā s'eyiṉum ikalkaruti
iṉṉās'ey yāmai talai.

853. Ikaleṉṉum evvanōy nīkkiṉ tavalillāt
tāvil viḷakkan tarum.

854. Iṉbattuḷ iṉbam payakkum ikaleṉṉum
tuṉbattuḷ tuṉban keḍiṉ.

855. Ikaledir s'āyndoḷuka vallārai yārē
mikalūkkum taṉmai yavar.

856. Ikaliṉ mikaliṉidu eṉpavaṉ vāḻkkai
tavalum keḍalum naṇittu.

857. Mikalmēval meypporuḷ kāṇār ikaṉmēval
iṉṉā aṟivi ṉavar.

858. Ikaliṟku etirs'āytal ākkam: ataṉai
mikalūkkiṉ ūkkumān kēḍu.

859. Ikalkāṇāṉ ākkam varunkāl ataṉai
mikalkāṇum kēḍu taraṟku.

860. Ikalāṉām iṉṉāta vellām: nakalāṉām
naṉṉayam eṉṉum s'eruḵku,

CHAPTER 86—ON DISCORD

851. Hatred is a foul disease that brings discord among men.

852. What if one does us harm out of hatred? It is the height of wisdom to resist not evil.

853. He who is rid of the full disease of hatred crowns himself with eternal glory.

854. It is the joy of joys to bury hatred, the evil of all evils.

855. Can any one overcome him who has conquered hatred?

856. Swift ruin awaits one who delights in discord.

857. Those who nourish hatred will never see the triumphant light of truth.

858. To fight against hatred is to save one's soul; to harbour it is to court one's own ruin.

859. Freedom from hatred is the sign of one's prosperity. Presence of hatred foreshadows decline of one's fortune.

860. From love springs the proud joy of a righteous life.

CHAPTER 87—PAKAI MĀṬCI

861. Valiyārkku maṟēṟṟal ōmpuka : ōmpā
meliyārmēl mēka pakai.

862. Aṉbilaṉ : āṉṟa tuṇaiyilaṉ : tāṉtuvvāṉ
eṉpariyum ētilāṉ tuppu.

863. Aññjum : aṟiyāṉ : amaivilaṉ : īkalāṉ
taññjam eḷiyaṉ pakaikku.

864. Nīngāṉ vekuḷi niṟaiyilaṉ eññāṉṟum
yānkaṇum yārkkum eḷitu.

865. Vaḻinōkkāṉ vāyppaṉa s'eyyāṉ paḻinōkkāṉ
paṇpilaṉ paṟṟāṟkku iṉitu.

866. Kāṇāc ciṉattāṉ kaḻiperum kāmattāṉ
pēṇāmai pēṇap paḍum.

867. Koḍuttun koḷalvēṇḍum maṉṟa aḍuttirundu
māṇāta s'eyvāṉ pakai.

868. Guṇaṉilaṉāyk kuṟṟam palavāyiṉ māṟṟārku
iṉaṉilaṉām ēmāp puḍaittu.

869. S'eṟuvārkkuc cēṇikavā iṉbam aṟivilā
aññjum pakaivarp peṟiṉ.

870. Kallāṉ vekuḷum s'iṟuporul eññāṉṟum
ollāṉai ollātu oḷi.

CHAPTER 87—ON ENMITY

861. Avoid hostility towards the powerful; do not cease from hostility towards the weak.

862. One devoid of love has neither the strength nor support. How can he stem the tide of the advancing foe?

863. He who is cowardly, ignorant, restless and niggardly, falls an easy prey to his enemy.

864. He who does not abstain from anger and has insufficient resources can be attacked by any one at any time.

865. He who does not walk in the right path or follow the rule, who is callous to public odium falls an easy victim to his enemies.

866. One can court the enmity of the blindly wrathful and the inordinately lustful.

867. It is good to get the enmity of one who is blind to one's purpose.

868. One who is void of virtue but full of vice invites the foe.

869. The cowardly and the foolish gladden the heart of the foe beyond measure.

870. Glory awaits one who does not exploit the ignorant.

CHAPTER 88—PAKAIT TIṞANTERITAL

871. Pakaiyeṉṉum paṇpi lataṉai oruvaṉ
nakaiyēyum vēṇḍaṟpāṟ ṟaṉṟu.

872. Villēr uḻavar pakaikoḷiṉun koḷḷaṟka
s'ollēr uḻavar pakai.

873. Ēmuṟ ṟavariṉum ēḻai tamiyaṉāyp
pallār pakaikoḷ pavaṉ.

874. Pakainaṭpāk koṇḍoḻukum paṇbuḍaiyāḷaṉ
takaimaikkaṉ taṅgiṟ ṟulaku.

875. Taṉtuṇai iṉṟāl pakaiiraṇḍāl tāṉoruvaṉ
iṉtuṇaiyāk koḷkavaṟṟiṉ oṉṟu.

876. Teṟiṉum tēṟā viḍiṉum aḻiviṉkaṇ
tēṟāṉ pakāaṉ viḍal.

877. Nōvaṟka nonda daṟiyārkku : mēvaṟka
meṉmai pakaivar akattu.

878. Vakaiyaṟindu taṟceytu taṟkāppa māyum
pakaivarkaṇ paṭṭa s'erukku.

879. Iḷaitāka muḷmaran kolka : kaḷaiyunar
kaikollum kāḻtta iḍattu.

880. Uyirppa uḷarallar maṉṟa s'eyirppavar
s'emmal s'itaikkalā tār,

CHAPTER 88—ON KNOWING THE ENEMY'S STRENGTH

871. One should not desire, even in a sportive mood, the evil known as enmity.

872. You may not fear the sword; but beware of the pen.

873. One who incurs the wrath of the enemy is blinder than the mad.

874. The world is under the sway of one who has the art of converting an enemy into a friend.

875. One who has no ally but two adversaries must befriend one of them.

876. In a dark hour assume a neutral attitude either to your known enemy or to an unknown foe.

877. Whisper not your troubles to friends who cannot divine them; betray not your weakness to your enemy.

878. Plan well your design and arm yourself with all the sinews of war.

879. Nip the thorn in the bud lest it should hurt the hands of those who seek to cut it when hardened into a tree.

880. He is one among the dead who fails to subdue his naughty foe.

CHAPTER 89—UṬPAKAI

881. Niḻalnīrum iṉṉāta iṉṉā: tamarnīrum
iṉṉāvām iṉṉā s'eyiṉ.

882. Vālpōl pakaivarai añjaṟka: añjuka
kēḷpōl pakaivar toṭarpu.

883. Uṭpakai yañjittaṟ kākka: ulaiviḍattu
maṭpakaiyiṉ māṇat teṟum.

884. Maṉammāṇā uṭpakai tōṉṟiṉ iṉammāṇā
ētam palavum tarum.

885. Uṟaṉmuṟaiyāṉ uṭpakai tōṉṟiṉ iṟaṉmuṟaiyāṉ
ētam palavum tarum.

886. Oṉṟāmai oṉṟiyār kaṇpaḍiṉ eññāṉṟum
poṉṟāmai oṉṟal aritu.

887. S'eppiṉ puṇarccipōl kūḍiṉum kūḍātē
uṭpakai uṟṟa kuḍi.

888. Aramporuta poṉpōlat tēyum uramporutu
uṭpakai uṟṟa kuḍi.

889. Eḷpaka vaṉṉa s'iṟumaittē yāyiṉum
uṭpakai uḷḷatām kēḍu.

890. Uḍampā ḍilātavar vāḻkkai kuḍankaruḷ
pāmpōḍu uḍaṉuṟain taṟṟu.

CHAPTER 89—INTERNAL FOES

881. Even shade and water, wholesome as they are, become pernicious where not needed; our kith and kin likewise are.

882. Be not afraid of open enemies with drawn swords; but beware of false friends.

883. Guard yourselves against your enemies from within. In your trying hour they will undermine your strength, like the potter's knife, cleaving the mind asunder.

884. The land is seething with dissensions when the foes from within, appear on the scene.

885. Many evils dark as death befall a king, when his own kith and kin sow dissensions in the land.

886. If kinsmen were to play to the traitor it would be difficult to escape death.

887. There will be no real union in a house divided. The apparent unity is like the appearance of the casket and the lid seen as one.

888. The family torn with internal dissensions dwindles in strength just like pure gold filed away by an iron file.

889. Internal hostility little as it is, like a tiny seed, hides within a mighty evil.

890. Dwelling among men of hidden hate is like dwelling in a hamlet which harbours a snake.

CHAPTER 90—PERIYĀRAIP PIḺAIYĀMAI

891. Āṟṟuvār āṟṟal ikaḻāmai pōṟṟuvār
pōṟṟaluḷ ellān tḻalai.

892. Periyāraip pēṇā toḻukiṉ periyārāl
pēra iḍumpai tarum.

893. Keḍalvēṇḍiṉ kēḷātu s'eyka aṭalvēṇḍiṉ
āṟṟu pavarkaṇ iḻukku.

894. Kūṟṟattai kaiyāl viḷittaṟṟāl āṟṟuvārkku
āṟṟātār iṉṉā s'eyal.

895. Yāṇḍucceṉ ṟiyāṇḍum uḷarākār venduppiṉ
vēndu s'erappaṭ ṭavar.

896. Eriyāl s'uḍappaḍiṉum uyvuṇḍām : uyyār
periyār piḻaittoḻuku vār.

897. Vakaimāṇḍa vāḻkkaiyum vāṉporuḷum eṉṉām
takaimāṇḍa takkār ceṟiṉ.

898. Kuṉṟaṉṉār kuṉṟa matippiṟ kuḍiyoḍu
niṉṟaṉṉār māyvar nilattu.

899. Ēntiya koḷkaiyār s'īriṉ iḍaimurindu
vēndaṉum vēndu keḍum.

900. Iṟandamainta s'ārpuḍaiyār āyiṉum uyyār
s'iṟandamainta s'īrār s'eṟiṉ.

CHAPTER 90—NOT CENSURING THE GREAT

891. Not to offend the mighty is the crowning means of shielding one self.

892. Lack of reverence for the great results in endless troubles.

893. To pick a quarrel with the mighty is to court one's own ruin.

894. Behold the weak trying to do harm to the mighty. It is like beckoning unto death.

895. Where is the refuge for one who incurs the wrath of the mighty monarch ?

896. There is just a chance of saving one self if one gets caught in a fire ; but there is no hope for men who insult the great.

897. What avails one's proof of prosperity and mighty riches if one rouses the wrath of the great.

898. The fury of the sages like the lofty hills destroys the great race of pure men of stable fortune.

899. Even the Lord of Heaven will be humbled from his throne if he rouses the wrath of men of mighty penance.

900. Even kings of ancient renown perish before the wrath of the great.

CHAPTER 91—PEṆVAḺIC CĒṚAL

901. Maṉaiviḻaivār māṇpayaṉ eytār: viṉaiviḻaivār
vēṇḍāp poruḷum atu.

902. Pēṇātu peṇviḻaivāṉ ākkam periyatōr
nāṇāka nāṇut tarum.

903. Illāḷkaṇ tāḻnta iyalpiṉmai eññāṉṟum
nallāruḷ nāṇut tarum.

904. Maṉaiyāḷai yañjum maṟumai yilāḷaṉ
viṉaiyāṇmai vīṟeytal iṉṟu.

905. Illāḷai yañjuvāṉ añjummaṟ ṟeññāṉṟum
nallārkku nalla seyal.

906. Imaiyāriṉ vāḻiṉum pāḍilarē illāḷ
amaiyārtōḷ añju pavar.

907. Peṇṇēval s'eytoḻukum āṇmaiyiṉ nāṇuḍaip
peṇṇē perumai yuḍaittu.

908. Naṭṭār kuṟaimuḍiyār naṉṟāṟṟār naṉṉutalāḷ
peṭṭāṅ koḻuku pavar.

909. Aṟaviṉaiyum āṉṟa poruḷum piṟaviṉaiyum
peṇṇēval s'eyvārkaṇ il.

910. Eṇs'ērnda neñjattu iḍaṉuḍaiyārkku eññāṉṟum
peṇs'ērndām pētaimai il.

CHAPTER 91—ON FOLLOWING WOMEN'S ADVICE

901. To follow one's wife's advice is to lose one's honour and fortune.

902. The wealth of a henpecked husband is a mere mockery to him.

903. The cowardice of one who submits to one's wife makes one shrink from the company of the good.

904. He who dreads his wife denies himself the joys of Heaven. Even his noble actions are held in scorn.

905. He who fears his wife fails in his offices to the good and the virtuous.

906. Those who are under the spell of their bamboo-shouldered bewitching wives cease to be men even though they are like Gods on earth.

907. More respectful is the bashfulness of a woman than the ignoble conduct of one who is a slave to one's wife.

908. An infatuated husband can never be a friend in need; nor can he hope to do virtuous deeds.

909. Pleasures of life are not for the henpecked husband.

910. Men of resolute will never commit the folly of slaving for women.

CHAPTER 92—VARAIVIṈ MAKAḶIR

911. Aṉpiṉ viḻaiyār poruḷviḻaiyum āytoḍiyār
iṉs'ol iḻukkut tarum.

912. Payaṉtūkkip paṇpuraikkum paṇpiṉ makaḷir
nayaṉtūkki naḷḷā viḍal.

913. Poruṭpeṇḍir poymmai muyakkam iruṭṭaṟaiyil
ētil piṇamtaḻīi aṟṟu.

914. Poruṭporuḷār puṉṉalam tōyār aruṭporuḷ
āyum aṟivi ṉavar.

915. Potunalattār puṉṉalam tōyār matinalattiṉ
māṇḍa aṟivi ṉavar.

916. Tannalam pārippār tōyār takais'erukkip
puṉṉalam pārippār tōḷ.

917. Niṟaineñjam illavar tōyvar piṟaneñjiṉ
pēṇip puṇarpavar tōḷ.

918. Āyum aṟiviṉar allārkku aṇangeṉpa
māya makaḷir muyakku.

919. Varaivilā māṇiḻaiyār meṉṟōḷ puraiyilāp
pūriyarkaḷ āḻum aḷaṟu.

920. Irumaṉap peṇḍirum kaḷḷum kavarum
tiruniīkkap paṭṭār toḍarpu.

CHAPTER 92—ON PUBLIC WOMEN

911. Honeyed words of public women who serve not for love but for money become gall and wormwood in the end.

912. Beware of public women sweet of tongue but greedy of gain.

913. Embracing false women bent on gain is like embracing a strange corpse in a dark room.

914. Men seeking the light of grace turn away in scorn from the fleshy delights of prostitutes.

915. Men of great wisdom care not for the barren pleasures of women who sell themselves for hire.

916. Men aspiring to fame do not long for the delights of women who sell themselves.

917. Only men of unruly desires go in search of the shoulders of women who sell themselves.

918. False women's embraces which only the ignorant desire are like the possession of evil spirits.

919. The soft shoulders of women who deck themselves for attraction are the hell into which undiscerning fools sink.

920. Double-tongued women, wine and dice are the allies of those abandoned by the goddess of fortune.

CHAPTER 93—KAḶḶUṆṆĀMAI

921. Uṭkap paḍāar oḷiiḷappar eññāṉṟum
kaṭkātal koṇḍoḷuku vār.

922. Uṇṇaṛka kaḷḷai: uṇiluṇka s'āṉṟōrāl
eṇṇap paḍavēṇḍā tār.

923. Īṉṟāḷ mukattēyum iṉṉātāl: eṉmaṟṟuc
cāṉṟōr mukattuk kaḷi.

924. Nāṇeṉṉum nallāḷ puṟankoḍukkum, kaḷeṉṉum
pēṇāp perunkuṟṟat tārkku.

925. Kaiyaṟi yāmai yuḍaittē poruḷkoḍuttu
meyyaṟi yāmai koḷal.

926. Tuñjiṉār s'ettāriṉ vēṟallar: eññāṉṟum
nañjuṇpār kaḷḷuṇ pavar.

927. Uḷḷoṟṟi uḷḷūr nakappaḍuvar eññāṉṟum
kaḷḷoṟṟik kaṇs'āy pavar.

928. Kaḷittaṟiyēn eṉpatu kaiviḍuka: neñjattu
oḷittadūum āṅkē mikum.

929. Kaḷittāṉaik kāraṇan kāṭṭutal kīḻnīrk
kuḷittāṉait tītturīi aṟṟu.

930. Kaḷḷuṇṇāp pōḻtil kaḷittāṉaik kāṇunkāl
uḷḷāṉkol uṇḍataṉ s'ōrvu.

CHAPTER 93—ON AVOIDING WINE

921. He who is addicted to wine can never strike fear in the heart of his foe ; nor can he retain his ancient splendour.

922. Do not drink wine, for a drunkard can never command the homage of the great.

923. Even an indulgent mother never puts up with a drunkard ; will the virtuous ever tolerate him ?

924. The good lady of modesty averts her face from him guilty of hateful drink.

925. To acquire forgetfulness at a price is indeed the fruit of past sin.

926. To be asleep is to be dead. To drink wine is to drink poison.

927. A drunkard who has lost his senses becomes an object of ridicule to his sober neighbours.

928. Let not a drunkard boast that he has not tasted wine ; for that which is hidden shows itself with greater force when drunk.

929. To reason a drunkard into his senses is like searching with a candle for one lost in deep waters.

930. If a drunkard in sober moments sees, another under the influence of wine, will he fail to realise his own state when drunk ?

CHAPTER 94—S'ŪTU

931. Vēṇḍaṟka veṉṟiḍiṉum s'ūtiṉai: veṉṟatūum
tūṇḍiṟpoṉ mīṉviḻunki yaṟṟu.

932. Oṉṟeyti nūṟuiḻakkum s'ūtarkkum uṇḍāṅkol
naṉṟeyti vāḻvatōr āṟu.

933. Uruḷāyam ōvātu kūṟiṉ poruḷāyam
pōoyp puṟamē paḍum.

934. S'iṟumai palas'eytu s'īraḻikkum s'ūtiṉ
vaṟumai taruvatoṉ ṟil.

935. Kavaṟum kaḻakamum kaiyum tarukki
ivaṟiyār illāki yār.

936. Akaḍuārār allal uḻappars'ū teṉṉum
mukaḍiyāl mūḍappaṭ ṭār.

937. Paḻakiya s'elvamum paṇpum keḍukkum
kaḻakattuk kālai pukiṉ.

938. Poruḷkeḍuttup poymēṟ koḷīi aruḷkeḍuttu
allal uḻappikkuñ cūtu.

939. Uḍais'elvam ūṇoḷi kalvieṉ ṟaintum
aḍaiyāvām āyan koḷiṉ.

940. Iḻattoṟūum kātalikkum s'ūtēpōl tuṉpam
uḻattoṟūum kātaṟ ṟuyir.

CHAPTER 94—ON GAMBLING

931. Do not desire to gamble even if you win; for your gain is like the bait to a fish.

932. Can gamblers who lose a hundred times before winning once ever dream of an upright life?

933. If one continually plays with the rolling dice one's riches desert one to enrich one's enemies.

934. Nothing brings on poverty more than gambling. If ruins one's fame and is the mother of all evils.

935. None but those who dream of dice and the gaming table will come to grief.

936. Torments of poverty and hell befall one who is seized by the demon of gambling.

937. Ceaseless gambling destroys one's ancestral wealth and fame.

938. Gambling destroys wealth, makes one play false, kills all virtues, and brings on distress.

939. A king whose hobby is gambling has neither raiment nor food, nor wealth nor renown nor learning.

940. In spite of all the ills of life we cling to it. In spite of all losses, a gambler clings to his dice.

CHAPTER 95—MARUNDU

941. Mikiṉum kuṟaiyiṉum nōys'eyyum nūlōr
valimutalā eṇṇiya mūṉṟu.

942. Marundeṉa vēṇḍāvām yākkaik karuntiyatu
aṟṟatu pōṟṟi uṇiṉ.

943. Aṟṟāl aḷavaṟin duṇka: ahduḍambu
peṟṟāṉ neḍituykkum āṟu.

944. Aṟṟa taṟindu kaḍaippiḍittu māṟalla
tuykka tuvarap pas'ittu.

945. Māṟupā ḍillāta uṇḍi maṟuttuṇṇiṉ
ūṟupā ḍillai uyirkku.

946. Iḻivaṟin duṇpāṉkaṇ iṉbampōl niṟkum
kaḻipēr iṟaiyāṉkaṇ nōy.

947. Tīyaḷa vaṉṟit teriyāṉ perituṇṇiṉ
nōyaḷa viṉṟip paḍum.

948. Nōynāḍi nōymutal nāḍi atutaṇikkum
vāynāḍi vāyppac ceyal.

949. Uṟṟāṉ aḷavum piṇiyaḷavum kālamum
kaṟṟāṉ karutic ceyal.

950. Uṟṟavaṉ tīrppāṉ marunduḻaic celvāṉeṉṟu
appālnāl kūṟṟē marundu.

END OF ANGAVIYAL

CHAPTER 95—ON MEDICINE

941. Overfeeding and underfeeding upset the three humours and cause disease,,says the physician.

942. There is no need for medicine if one eats with appetite.

943. Let there be measure and moderation in eating. It leads to long life.

944. Eat wholesome food when you feel hungry.

945. No disease attacks the person who eats with moderation the food which agrees with him.

946. Health dwells in a man of temperance, disease invades a glutton.

947. Countless are the ills that befall a glutton.

948. Diagnose the disease, find out its cure after tracing its root and apply the proper remedy.

949. Let the learned physician know the nature of the patient and the duration of ailment and then treat.

950. The science of medicine deals with the patient, the physician, the medicine and the recipe.

END OF ANGAVIYAL

OḺIPIYAL

CHAPTER 96—KUḌIMAI

951. Iṟpiṟantār kaṇ'alla tillai iyalpākac
ceppamum nāṇum orunku.

952. Oḻukkamum vāymaiyum nāṇumim mūṉṟum
iḻukkār kuḍippiṟan tār.

953. Nakaiyīkai iṉs'ol ikaḻāmai nāṉkum
vakaiyeṉba vāymaik kuḍikku.

954. Aḍukkiya kōḍi peṟiṉum kuḍippiṟantār
kuṉṟuva s'eytal ilar.

955. Vaḻanguva duḷvīḻndak kaṇṇum paḻankuḍi
paṇpiṟ ṟalaippirital iṉṟu.

956. Calampaṟṟic cālpila s'eyyārmā s'aṟṟa
kulampaṟṟi vāḻtumeṉ pār.

957. Kuḍippiṟantār kaṇviḷankum kuṟṟam vis'umpiṉ
matikkaṇ maṟuppōl uyarndu.

958. Nalattiṉkaṇ nāriṉmai tōṉṟiṉ avaṉaik
kulattiṉkaṇ aiyap paḍum.

959. Nilattil kiḍantamai kālkāṭṭum : kāṭṭum
kulattil piṟandārvāyc col.

960. Nalamvēṇḍiṉ nāṇuḍaimai vēṇḍum : kulamvēṇḍiṉ
vēṇḍuka yārkkum paṇivu.

SECTION—III: THE RESIDUE

CHAPTER 96—ON NOBLE LINEAGE

951. Probity and a sense of shame are virtues innate only in men of noble lineage.

952. Men of noble descent never forsake good conduct, truthfulness and modesty.

953. A cheerful countenance, charity, soft words and sweet learning all these characterise men of noble birth.

954. Men of noble birth never stoop to mean acts, though they may thereby gain untold riches.

955. A family of ancient dignity never fails of its charity even when fallen on evil days.

956. Those who walk in the untarnished traditions of their noble family never do wrong even in poverty.

957. Dark as the spot of the Moon in the sky doth the stain of the noble family loom large.

958. The world suspects the noble lineage of one who lacks in sympathy.

959. The plants are quite racy of the soil. The words of men of high birth betoken their ancestral dignity.

960. Out of modesty springs one's greatness. Out of humility rises the honour of family.

CHAPTER 97—MĀṈAM

961. Iṉṟi amaiyāc ciṟappiṉa vāyiṉum
kuṉṟa varupa viḍal.

962. S'īriṉum s'iralla s'eyyārē s'īroḍu
pērāṇmai vēṇḍu pavar.

963. Perukkattu vēṇḍum paṇital s'eṟiya
s'urukkattu vēṇḍum uyarvu.

964. Talaiyiṉ iḻinda mayiraṉaiyar māndar
nilaiyiṉ iḻindak kaḍai.

965. Kuṉṟiṉ aṉaiyārum kuṉṟuvar kuṉṟuva
kuṉṟi aṉaiya s'eyiṉ.

966. Pukaḻiṉṟāl puttēḷnāṭ ṭuyyātāl eṉmaṟṟu
ikaḻvārpiṉ s'eṉṟu nilai.

967. Oṭṭārpiṉ s'eṉṟoruvaṉ vāḻtaliṉ annilaiyē
keṭṭāṉ eṉappaḍutal naṉṟu.

968. Marundōmaṟ ṟuṉōmbum vāḻkkai peruntakaimai
pīḍaḻiya vanda viḍattu.

969. Mayirnīppiṉ vāḻāk kavarimā aṉṉār
uyirnīppar māṉam variṉ.

970. Iḷivariṉ vāḻāta māṉam uḍaiyār
oḷitoḻu dēttum ulaku.

CHAPTER 97—ON HONOUR

961. Reject mean actions, even if they bring glory in their turn.

962. Those who desire honour and name will not do mean things in their thirst for glory.

963. During prosperity practise humility. Even in adversity keep dignity.

964. Men fallen from a high estate are like the hair fallen from the head.

965. Even a trivial mean act will drag down a man from the hill top of his eminence.

966. Of what use is servility to one who despises you? It brings neither fame nor does it show the path to heaven.

967. Better to die in poverty than to be servile to one that scorns you.

968. When one's honour is ruined, will the life that sustains the body confer immortality?

969. He whose honour is at stake lays down his life like the Yak that is shorn of its single hair.

970. The world sings in praise of those noble persons who prefer death to dishonour.

CHAPTER 98—PERUMAI

971. Oḷiyoruvaṛ kuḷḷa veṛukkai iḷiyoruvaṛku
ahdiṛandu vāḻtṉm eṉal.

972. Piṛappokkum ellā uyirkkum s'iṛappovvā
s'eytoḻil vēṛṛumai yāṉ.

973. Mēlirundum mēlallār mēlallar : kīḻirundum
kīḻallār kīḻal lavar.

974. Orumai makaḷirē pōlap perumaiyum
taṉṉaittāṉ koṇḍoḷukiṉ uṇḍu.

975. Perumai uḍaiyavar āṛṛuvār āṛṛiṉ
arumai uḍaiya s'eyal.

976. S'iṛiyār uṇarcciyuḷ illaip periyāraip
pēṇikkoḷ vēmeṉṉum nōkku.

977. Iṛappē purinda toḻiṛṛām s'iṛappumtāṉ
s'īral lavarkaṇ paḍiṉ.

978. Paṇiyumām eṉṛum perumai : s'iṛumai
aṇiyumām taṉṉai viyandu.

979. Perumai perumitam iṉmai : s'iṛumai
perumitam ūrndu viḍal.

980. Aṛṛam maṛaikkum perumai : s'iṛumaitāṉ
kuṛṛamē kūṛi viḍum.

CHAPTER 98—ON GREATNESS

971. The glory of life is to achieve greatness. The poverty of life is to be lost to all glory.

972. It is not birth but deeds that mark men.

973. One is not great because of one's birth in a noble family; one is not low because of one's low birth.

974. Greatness springs from one's own good conduct preserved like the sacred honour of a woman.

975. Greatness achieves things difficult for others.

976. Littleness feels no reverence for the great.

977. Littleness is proud of its virtues.

978. Greatness is all humility; littleness is all arrogance.

979. Greatness is not conscious of its worth. Littleness is rooted in pride.

980. Greatness hides the faults of others; littleness trumpets their faults alone.

CHAPTER 99—S'ĀṈṞĀṆMAI

981. Kaḍaṉeṉpa nallavai ellām kaḍaṉaṟindu
s'āṉṟāṇmai mēṟkoḷ pavarkku.

982. Guṇanalam s'āṉṟōr nalaṉē piṟanalam
ennalat tuḷḷadūum aṉṟu.

983. Aṉbunāṇ oppuravu kaṇṇōṭṭam vāymaiyōḍu
aindus'ālpu .ūṉṟiya tūṇ.

984. Kollā nalattatu nōṉmai: piṟartīmai
s'ollā nalattatu s'ālpu.

985. Āṟṟuvār āṟṟal paṇital: atus'āṉṟōr
māṟṟārai māṟṟum paḍai.

986. S'ālpiṟkuk kaṭṭaḷai yādeṉil tōlvi
tulaiallār kaṇṇum koḷal.

987. Iṉṉāsey dārkkum iṉiyavē s'eyyākkāl
eṉṉa payattatō s'ālpu.

988. Iṉmai oṟuvaṟ kiḷivaṉṟu s'ālpeṉṉum
tiṇmaiyuṇ ḍākap peṟiṉ.

989. Ūḷi peyariṉum tāmpeyarār s'āṉṟāṇmaikku
āḷi yeṉappaḍu vār.

990. S'āṉṟavar s'āṉṟāṇmai kuṉṟiṉ irunilamtāṉ
tāṅgātu maṉṉō poṟai.

CHAPTER 99—ON GOOD CONDUCT

981. All virtues dwell in one who is alive to one's nobility of conduct.

982. Good conduct is the virtue of the great; all other things are but dross.

983. Love, modesty, impartiality, sympathy and truthfulness are the five pillars of nobility.

984. Penance kills not, nobility slanders not.

985. Humility is the strength of the great. It is the weapon that disarms the foe.

986. The touchstone of nobility is to accept defeat even at the hands of inferiors.

987. What profits one's nobility if good is not done even to those who do harm?

988. Poverty is no disgrace to one of enduring nobility.

989. The sea may recede but noble men will remain steadfast.

990. Were the nobility of the noble to shrink, the vast firm earth would totter.

CHAPTER 100—PAṆBUḌAIMAI

991. Eṇpadattāl eytal eḷiteṉba yārmāṭṭum
paṇbuḍaimai ,yeṉṉum vaḷakku.

992. Aṉbuḍaimai āṉṟa kuḍippiṟattal ivvirandum
paṇbuḍaimai yeṉṉum vaḷakku.

993. Uṟuppottal makkaḷop paṉṟāl veṟuttakka
paṇbottal oppatām oppu.

994. Nayaṉoḍu naṉṟi purinda payaṉuḍaiyār
paṇbupā rāṭṭum ulaku.

995. Nakaiyuḷḷum iṉṉā dikaḷcci : pakaiyuḷḷum
paṇbuḷa pāḍaṟivār māṭṭu.

996. Paṇbuḍaiyārp paṭṭuṇ ḍulakam : aduiṉṟēl
maṇpukku māyvatu maṇ.

997. Arampōlum kūrmaiya rēṉum marampōlvar
makkaḷpaṇ billā tavar.

998. Naṇpāṟṟār āki nayamila s'eyvārkkum
paṇpāṟṟār ātal kaḍai.

999. Nakalvallar allārkku māiru ñālam
pakalumpāl paṭṭaṉ ṟiruḷ.

1000. Paṇbillāṉ peṟṟa peruñcelvam naṉpāl
kalamtīmai yāltirin daṟṟu.

CHAPTER 100—ON COURTESY

991. Be cautious and easy of access. You will command the homage of the world.

992. Courtesy springs from love and noble lineage.

993. Mere physical features do not rank with men but only courtesy makes them ascend the scale.

994. The world respects the courtesy of those who are just and willing to do good.

995. Do not mock at others even in a sportive mood. There is virtue in being courteous even to a foe.

996. The world is built on the wisdom of the noble and the good; but for them the entire world would be a heap of ruins.

997. Of what avail is one's intelligence keen as the edge of the chistle ? One is with the socks and gloves if one is not affable.

998. To be failing in one's courtesy even to one's foe is sin.

999. Even the wide world darkens at noon to the sullen who fails to gladden the hearts of men.

1000. Of what use is the wealth of the discourteous ? It is like good milk spoilt by an unclean vessel.

CHAPTER 101—NAṈṞIYIL S'ELVAM

1001. Vaittāṉvāy s'āṉṟa perumporuḷ ahduṇṇāṉ
s'ettāṉ: s'eyaḳḳiḍanda dil.

1002. Poruḷāṉām ellāmeṉ ṟiyā tivaṟum
maruḷāṉām māṇāp piṟappu.

1003. Īṭṭam ivaṟi is'aivēṇḍā āḍavar
tōṟṟam nilakkup poṟai.

1004. Eccameṉ ṟaṉeṇṇum kollō oruvarāl
naccap paḍāa tavaṉ.

1005. Koḍuppadūum tuyppadūum illārk kaḍukkiya
kōḍiuṇ ḍāyiṉum il.

1006. Ētam peruñcelvam tāṉtuvvāṉ takkārkkoṉṟu
ītal iyalpilā tāṉ.

1007. Aṟṟārkkoṉ ṟāṟṟātāṉ s'elvam mikanalam
peṟṟāḷ tamiyaḷmūt taṟṟu.

1008. Naccap paḍātavaṉ s'elvam naḍuūruḷ
naccu marampaḻut taṟṟu.

1009. Aṉboriit taṟceṟ ṟaṟamnōkkā dīṭṭiya
oṇporuḷ koḷvār piṟar.

1010. S'īruḍaic celvar s'iṟutuṉi māri
vaṟamkūrn daṉaiya duḍaittu.

CHAPTER 101—ON UNPROFITABLE WEALTH

1001. He who does not make use of his hoarded wealth is really dead, though alive; for he cannot do anything great.

1002. The birth of a ghost awaits a miser who thinks he gains everything by hoarding wealth.

1003. He who prefers mere accumulation of wealth to glory is a burden unto the earth.

1004. What awaits one if one cannot win the affections of others?

1005. Of what avail is the untold wealth of one who neither gives nor enjoys it?

1006. Abundance of wealth is not a blessing but a curse to one who can neither enjoy it nor spend it on the deserving.

1007. The wealth that is not spent on the needy is as barren as the withering charm of a spinster.

1008. The wealth of a miser is like the fruit of a poison-tree in the heart of a village.

1009. Strangers inherit the great wealth of a miser who neither enjoys it nor gives.

1010. The short-lived poverty of the generous rich is the drought of rain-laden clouds.

CHAPTER 102—NĀṆUḌAIMAI

1011. Karumattāl nāṇutal nāṇut tirunutal
nallavar nāṇup piṟa.

1012. Ūṇuḍai eccam uyirkkellām vēṟalla:
nāṇuḍaimai māndar s'iṟappu.

1013. Ūṉaik kuṟitta uyirellām: nāṇeṉṉum
naṉmai kuṟittatu s'ālpu.

1014. Aṇiaṉṟō nāṇuḍaimai s'āṉṟōrkku ahdiṉṟēl
piṇiaṉṟō pīḍu naḍai.

1015. Piṟarpaḻiyum tampaḻiyum nāṇuvār nāṇukku
uṟaipati eṉṉum ulaku.

1016. Nāṇvēli koḷḷātu maṉṉō viyaññālam
pēṇalar mēlā yavar.

1017. Nāṇāl uyirait tuṟappar uyirpporuṭṭāl
nāṇtuṟavār nāṇāḷ pavar.

1018. Piṟarnāṇat takkatu tāṉnāṇāṉ āyiṉ
aṟamnāṇat takka duḍaittu.

1019. Kulams'uḍum koḷkai piḻaippiṉ: nalams'uḍum
nāṇiṉmai niṉṟak kaḍai.

1020. Nāṇakat tillār iyakkam marappāvai
nāṇāl uyirmaruṭṭi yaṟṟu.

CHAPTER 102—ON MODESTY

1011. True modesty shrinks from littleness. All other forms of modesty are womanish.

1012. Common to all human beings are food and clothing and other necessaries of life. But what distinguishes them is modesty.

1013. Man clings to his body. The noble clings to modesty.

1014. Disgraceful is the painted pomp of the life of the immodest.

1015. The world finds the very abode of modesty in one who dreads one's infamy and that of others.

1016. The great prefer modesty to the riches of the world.

1017. Better retain modesty than cling to life. The noble would rather die than lose modesty.

1018. One who does not shrink from what others blush at, knows no righteousness.

1019. Lack of decorum disgraces a home; lack of modesty destroys everything good.

1020. The activity of those lacking in modesty is like that of a marionette.

CHAPTER 103—KUḌI S'EYALVAKAI

1021. Karumam s'eyaoruvaṉ kaitūvēṉ eṉṉum
perumaiyil pīḍuḍaiya dil.

1022. Āḷviṉaiyum āṉṟa aṟivum eṉairaṇḍiṉ
nīḷviṉaiyāl nīḷum kuḍi.

1023. Kuḍis'eyval eṉṉum oruvaṟkut teyvam
maḍitaṟṟut tāṉmun duṟum.

1024. S'ūḻāmal tāṉē muḍiveydum tamkuḍiyait
tāḻā duñaṟṟu pavarkku.

1025. Kuṟṟam ilaṉāyk kuḍis'eydu vāḻvāṉaic
s'uṟṟamāc cuṟṟum ulaku.

1026. Nalāṇmai eṉba doruvarkkut tāṉpiṟanda
ilāṇmai ākkik kolal.

1027. Amarakattu vaṉkaṇṇar pōlat tamarakattum
āṟṟuvār mēṟṟē poṟai.

1028. Kuḍis'eyvārk killaip paruvam: maḍis'eytu
māṉam karutak keḍum.

1029. Iḍumbaikkē koḷkalam kollō kuḍumbattaik
kuṟṟam maṟaippāṉ uḍambu.

1030. Iḍukkaṇkāl koṉṟiḍa vīḻum aḍuttūṉṟum
nallāḷ ilāta kuḍi.

CHAPTER 103—ON EXALTING ONE'S FAMILY

1021. Nothing is more exalted and manly than one's ceaseless toil to uplift one's own family.

1022. Manly effort and ripe wisdom exalt one's family.

1023. Even God girds up His loins in the service of one who strives for the glory of one's family.

1024. Success comes unbidden to one who exalts one's family with unremitting toil.

1025. The world becomes kin to one who leads an unblemished householder's life.

1026. What is true manliness except perfect ordering of the house for its own glory?

1027. The brunt of the battle falls on the victorious; the burden of the family on the competent few.

1028. To pure householders there is no cessation of work. One's false prestige leads to the ruin of one's family.

1029. Is he who protects his family from the ills of life a mere vessel of suffering?

1030. The axe of adversity falls on the family which has no noble son to shield it.

CHAPTER 104—UḺAVU

1031. S'uḻanṟumērp piṉṉa dulakam ataṉāl
uḻandum uḻavē talai.

1032. Uḻuvār ulakattārk kāṇiah dāṟṟādu
eḻuvārai ellām poṟuttu.

1033. Uḻutuṇḍu vāḻvārē vāḻvārmaṟ ṟellām
toḻutuṇḍu piṉs'el pavar.

1034. Palakuḍai nīḻalum tamkuḍaikkīḻk kāṇpar
alakuḍai nīḻalavar.

1035. Iravār irappārkkoṉ ṟīvar karavātu
kais'eytūṇ mālai yavar.

1036. Uḻaviṉār kaimmaḍankiṉ illai viḻaivatūum
viṭṭēmeṉ pārkku nilai.

1037. Toḍippuḻutı kahcā uṇakkin piḍitteruvum
vēṇḍātu s'ālap paḍum.

1038. Ērinum naṉṟāl eruviḍutal kaṭṭapiṉ
nīrinum naṉṟataṉ kāppu.

1039. S'ellāṉ kiḻavaṉ iruppiṉ nilampulandu
illāḷiṉ ūḍi viḍum.

1040. Ilameṉ ṟasaii yiruppāraik kāṇiṉ
nilameṉṉum nallāḷ ṇakum,

CHAPTER 104—ON AGRICULTURE

1031. After vain wanderings in search of callings the world returned to the plough.

1032. Husbandmen are the sheet-anchor of the world; for on them depend lives of others.

1033. Only the husbandmen live; all others subsist on their toil.

1034. It is the husbandmen that bring the might of the kings under the sway of their own sovereign.

1035. A toiling peasant never begs but gives.

1036. Even the anchorite ceases from penance if husbandmen sit with their hands folded.

1037. Let the land be allowed to dry with dust. Even a handful of manure is not needed for a good harvest.

1038. After weeding, let the land be guarded, for more important than water is the protection of crops.

1039. The land neglected by its owner puts on the appearance of a sulky woman abandoned by her lord.

1040. Mother earth laughs in scorn at those who plead poverty.

CHAPTER 105—NALKURAVU

1041. Iṉmaiyiṉ iṉṉāda diyādeṉiṉ iṉmaiyiṉ
iṉmaiyē iṉṉā datu.

1042. Iṉmai eṉaoru pāvi maṟumaiyum
immaiyum iṉṟi varum.

1043. Tolvaravum tōlum keḍukkum tokaiyāka
Nalkura veṉṉum nas'ai.

1044. Ilpiṟandār kaṇṇēyum iṉmai iḷivaṇda
s'olpiṟakkum s'ōrvu tarum.

1045. Nalkura veṉṉum iḍumbaiyuḷ palkurait
tuṉbankaḷ s'eṉṟu paḍum.

1046. Naṟporuḷ naṉkuṇarndu s'olliṉum nalkūrndār
s'oṟporuḷ s'ōrvu paḍum.

1047. Aṟams'ārā nalkura viṉṟatā yāṉum
piṟaṉpōla nōkkap paḍum.

1048. Iṉṟum varuvatu kollō nerunalum
koṉṟatu pōlum nirappu.

1049. Neruppiṉuḷ tuñjalum ākum nirappiṉuḷ
yātoṉṟum kaṇpā ḍaritu.

1050. Tuppura villār tuvarat tuṟavāmai
uppiṟkum kāḍikkum kūṟṟu.

CHAPTER 105—ON POVERTY

1041. There is no greater evil than poverty.

1042. Poverty is an evil which blasts at once the joys of earth and of heaven.

1043. Poverty which springs of avarice ruins one's ancestry and its fair name.

1044. Dejection due to poverty makes the noble utter the language of the base.

1045. Poverty in itself an evil is the mother of all ills.

1046 The words of the poor, though born of experience and wisdom are not listened to.

1047. Even a mother turns her back on one whose poverty is devoid of probity.

1048. Oh, how I dread it! Will that beggary that almost killed me yesterday assail me today also?

1049. One may sleep in the midst of scorching fire. But the poverty-stricken know no sleep.

1050. The indigent that do not renounce the world batten on other man's salt and porridge.

CHAPTER 106—IRAVU

1051. Irakka irattakkār kāṇin karappin
avarpaḷi tampaḷi anṛu.

1052. Inbam oruvaṛ kirattal irandavai
tunbam uṛāa varin.

1053. Karappilā neñjin kaḍanaṛivār munninṛu
irappumōr ēer uḍaittu.

1054. Irattalum idalē pōlum karattal
kanavilum tēṛṛātār māṭṭu.

1055. Karappilār vaiyakat tuṇmaiyāl kaṇnin
ṛirappavar mēlkoḷ vatu.

1056. Karappiḍumbai illāraik kāṇin nirappiḍumbai
ellām orunku keḍum.

1057. Ikaḻndeḷḷā dīvāraik kāṇin makiḻnduḷḷam
uḷḷum uvappa duḍaittu.

1058. Irappārai illāyin īrmkaṇmā ñālam
marappāvai s'enṛuvan daṛṛu.

1059. Īvarkaṇ enuṇḍām tōṛṛam irandukōḷ
mēvār ilāak kaḍai.

1060. Irappān vekuḷāmai vēṇḍum nirappiḍumbai
tānēyum s'ālum kari.

CHAPTER 106—ON BEGGING

1051. Beg if you meet people who can give. If they refuse, it is their fault, not yours.

1052. Begging would be pleasant to one if one were to achieve one's object without causing pain.

1053. There is a grace even in begging of one noble and generous of heart.

1054. Begging is endowed with all the grace of giving when the noble guest does not fail of his gifts even in dreams.

1055. There is beggary because of persons touched by its very presence.

1056. All the indignities of begging vanish in the presence of the truly generous who know not the sin of withholding gifts.

1057. Mendicancy inwardly rejoices in the bounty of the generous free of scorn.

1058. Were there to be no mendicancy the vast world would be peopled with men moving like dolls.

1059. If there be no beggars in the world, will there be any glory for the bountiful?

1060. Do not chafe against the hunks for inevitable is the pain of poverty.

CHAPTER 107—IRAVACCAM

1061. Karavā duvantīyum kaṇaṉṉār kaṇṇum
iravāmai kōḍi uṟum.

1062. Irandum uyirvāḻtal vēṇḍiṉ parandu
keḍuka ulakiyaṟṟi yāṉ.

1063. Iṉmai iḍumpai irandutīr vāmeṉṉum
vaṉmaiyiṉ vaṉpāṭṭa dil.

1064. Iḍamellām koḷḷāt takaittē iḍamillāk
kālum iravollāccālpu.

1065. Teḷnīr aḍupuṟkai āyiṉum tāḷtandadu
uṇṇaliṉ ūṅgiṉiya dil.

1066. Āviṟku nīreṉ ṟirappiṉum nāviṟku
iraviṉ iḷivanda dil.

1067. Irappaṉ irappārai ellām irappiṉ
karappār iravaṉmiṉ eṉṟu.

1068. Iraveṉṉum ēmāppil tōṇi karaveṉṉum
pārtākkap pakku viḍum.

1069. Iravuḷḷa uḷḷam urukum: karavuḷḷa
uḷḷatūum iṉṟik keḍum.

1070. Karappavark kiyāṅkoḷikkum kollō irappavar
sollāḍap pōom uyir.

CHAPTER 107—ON FEAR OF BEGGING

1061. A million times blessed is he who refrains from begging even from the generous delighting in charity.

1062. May the creator of the world perish if he has ordained life only through mendicancy.

1063. There is no greater folly than the thought of wiping out poverty by beggary.

1064. The greatness of refusing to beg even in adversity transcends the glory of the world.

1065. Nothing is sweeter than the thin porridge earned by the sweat of one's brow.

1066. It is a heinous sin to beg for water even for a cow crying of thirst.

1067. I implore beggars not to beg of people who hide their wealth.

1068. The unavailing canoe of begging gets wrecked on the rock of refusal.

1069. The mere thought of begging melts one's heart. It breaks at one's denial.

1070. A rebuff takes the life out of the beggar. But can the deceitful escape death?

CHAPTER 108—KAYAMAI

1071. Makkaḷē pōlvar kayavar avaraṉṉa
oppā riyānkaṇḍa dil.

1072. Naṉṟaṟi vāriṟ kayavar tiruvuḍaiyar
neñjat tavalam ilar.

1073. Tēvar aṉaiyar kayavar avarumtām
mēvaṉa s'eytoḻuka lāṉ.

1074. Akappaṭṭi āvāraik kāṇiṉ avariṉ
mikappaṭṭuc cemmākkum kīḻ.

1075. Accamē kīḻkaḷa dācāram eccam
avāuṇḍēl uṇḍām s'iṟitu.

1076. Aṟaipaṟai aṉṉar kayavartām kēṭṭa
maṟaipiṟark kuytturaikka lāṉ.

1077. Īrnkai vitirār kayavar koḍiṟuḍaikkum
kūṉkaiyar allā tavarkku.

1078. S'ollap payaṉpaḍuvar s'āṉṟōr karumpupōl
kollap payaṉpaḍun kīḻ.

1079. Uḍuppadūum uṇpadūum kāṇiṉ piṟarmēl
vaḍukkāṇa vaṟṟākum kīḻ.

1080. Eṟṟir kuriyar kayavar? oṉ ṟuṟṟakkāl
viṟṟaṟ kuriyar viraintu.

END OF PORUṬPĀL

CHAPTER 108—ON MEANNESS

1071. Ignoble men are only touched with human shapes. Rare indeed are such specimens.

1072. Blessed are the base who are ignorant of the good. Verily they are never ill at ease.

1073. Mean men resemble unruly gods, for they know no law.

1074. The mean fought their superiority among men baser than them.

1075. Fear and desire rule the conduct of the base.

1076. The base are like the drum for they noise abroad the secrets of men.

1077. The base part with their crumbs only to a clenched hand.

1078. Even the least cry of distress touches the heart of the good; but squeezing goodness out of the vile is like crushing the sugar-cane.

1079. The base envy others in their food and clothing and slander them.

1080. What are the base men fit for? They hasten only to sell themselves in adversity.

END OF PORUṬPĀL

KĀMATTUPPĀL

SECTION I. KAḶAVIYAL

CHAPTER 109—TAKAIYAṆANGUṚUTTAL

1081. Aṇangukol ? āiymayil kollo ? kaṇangulai
mātarkol ? mālumeṉ neñju.

1082. Nōkkiṉāḷ nōkkedir nōkkudal tākkaṇangu
tāṇaikkoṇḍaṉṉa tuḍaittu.

1083. Paṇḍaṟiyēṉ kūṟṟeṉ padaṉai : iṉi aṟindēṉ
peṇtakaiyāl pēramark kaṭṭu.

1084. Kaṇḍār uyir uṇṇum toṟṟattāl peṇtakaip
pēdaikku amarttaṉa kaṇ.

1085. Kūṟṟamō ! kaṇṇō ? piṇaiyō ! Maḍavaral
nōkkamim mūṉṟum uḍaittu.

1086. Koḍum puruvam kōḍā maṟaippiṉ naḍungu ajñar
s'eyyala maṉivaḷ kaṇ.

1087. Kaḍāk kaḷiṟṟiṉmēl kaṇpaḍām mātar
paṭāa mulaimēl tukil.

1088. Oṇṇutaṟko ouḍaindatē jñāṭpiṉuḷ
naṇṇārum uḍkumeṉ pīḍu.

1089. Piṇaiēr maḍanōkkum nāṇum uḍaiyāṭku
aṇievaṉō ēdila tandu.

1090. Uṇḍārkaṇ allatu aḍunaṟāk kāmampōl
kaṇḍār makiḷs'eydal iṉṟu.

SECTION I. THE SECRET UNION

CHAPTER 109—ON LOVER'S DISTRACTION

1081. Is this a goddess fair? Or is it a rare peacock? Or, is it a mortal with heavy ear-rings? My mind is perplexed in the extreme.

1082. The glance she returns for mine resembles that of a terrible goddess leading an army.

1083. The god of death I never knew. Now I behold him in the shape of this woman with battling eyes.

1084. The cruel eyes of this woman seem to devour the lives of those on whom they fall.

1085. Oh, how the death-dealing antelope-eyes of the lady charm and puzzle me!

1086. Her cruel eyes, had they not been shaded by her brows, would have made me quail and shudder.

1087. The garment over the ample swell of her bosom is like the cloth on the face of a wild elephant.

1088. My might which has struck terror in the heart of the foe who has only heard of my prowess lies overthrown before her splendid face.

1089. What need of ornament has this lady of modesty, adorned with the glances of an antelope?

1090. Wine intoxicates the person when only drunk but love inebriates the soul even by a mere look.

CHAPTER 110—KUṚIPPAṚITAL

1091. Irunōkku ivaḷ uṇkaṇ uḷḷatu ; orunōkku
nōynōkku : oṉṟu annōy marundu.

1092. Kaṇkaḷavu koḷḷum s'iṟu nōkkam kāmattil
s'empākam aṉṟu: peridu.

1093. Nōkkiṉāḷ : nōkki iṟaiññjiṉāḷ : ahdavaḷ
yāppiṉuḷ aṭṭiya nīr.

1094. Yāṉnōkkum kālai nilaṉ nōkkum ; nōkkākkāl
tāṉnōkki mella nakum.

1095. Kuṟikkoṇḍu nokkāmai allāl orukaṇ
s'iṟakkaṇittāḷ pola nakum.

1096. Uṟāa tavarpōl s'oliṉum s'eṟāars'ol
ollai uṇarap paṭum.

1097. S'eṟāacciṟus'ollum s'eṟṟārpōl nōkkum
uṟārpoṉṟu uṟṟār kuṟippu.

1098. as'aiyiyaṟku uṇḍāṇḍu ōr ēyar : yāṉ nōkkap
pas'aiyiṉaḷ paiya nakum.

1099. Yētilār polap podunōkku nōkkutal
kādalār kaṇṇē uḷa.

1100. Kaṇṇōḍu kaṇṇiṇai nōkkokkiṉ vāiccoṟkaḷ
eṉṉa payaṉum ila.

CHAPTER 110—READING LOVE'S SIGNS

1091. The glances of her collirium-painted eyes have a double sway. One wounds and the other heals.

1092. More telling than her actual embrace are her stealthy love looks.

1093. She gazed and gazed but she became shy and her bashful look has nurtured the plant of love between us.

1094. She casts her shy look on earth when I gaze at her; but if I turn aside, she glances at me with a gentle smile.

1095. Without looking straight at me, with furtive glances she smiles inwardly.

1096. Though her words are as harsh as those of a stranger, they betoken only love.

1097. The pretended angry look and the bitter-sweet word of the beloved are like those of a stranger. Surely these are but the masks of her love.

1098. When I look beseechingly at her she returns a gentle smile. Oh, what bewitching charm fills the tender maid's look.

1099. Oh, what an indifferent air do the lovers assume! They look at each other as if they were strangers.

1100. Of what avail are words when eyes speak to eyes and heart whispers unto heart.

CHAPTER 111—PUṆARCCI MAKIḺTAL

1101. Kaṇḍu keṭṭuṇḍuyirttu uṟṟaṟiyum aimpulaṉum
oṇtoḍi kaṇṇe uḷa.

1102. Piṇikku marundu piṟamaṉ aṇiyıḷāi
taṉnōykkut tānē marundu.

1103. Tāmvīḻvār meṉtoḷ tuyilin yiṉitukol
tāmaraik kaṇṇāṉ ulaku?

1104. Nīngil terūum: kurukumkāl taṇeṉṉum
tīyāṇḍup peṟṟāḷ ivaḷ.

1105. Vēṭṭāpoḷutiṉ avai avai pōlumē
tōṭṭār kaduppināḷ toḷ.

1106. Uṟutōṟū uyir talirppat tīṇḍalāl pēdaikku
amīḻdiṉ iyaṉdraṇa toḷ.

1107. Tammil irundu tamatupāt tuṇḍaṟṟāl
ammā arivai muyakku.

1108. Vīḻum iruvarkku iṉitē vaḷiyiḍai
pōḻappaḍā muyakku.

1109. Ūḍal uṇartal puṇardal, ivai kāmam
kūiyār peṟṟa payaṉ.

1110. Aṟitōṟu aṟīyāmai kaṅḍaṟṟāl kāmam
s'eritoṟum sēyiḻai māṭṭu.

CHAPTER 111—THE ECSTACY OF LOVE'S UNION

1101. All the pleasures that the five senses give us are garnered in this lady with glittering bracelets. What a thrill she gives me!

1102. The remedy for a disease lies not in the disease but in some healing balm; but not so the loved one who is at once the disease and the cure for the pangs of love.

1103. Are the pleasures of the world of the lotus-eyed lord sweeter than reclining on the soft shoulder of the beloved?

1104. This lady has a fire which burns me with passion when I am away; but it cools down when I see her. Can any one say where she has acquired this power?

1105. Like the dreams of pleasures sought, the embrace of this sweet-shouldered, flower-decked maiden gives me untold pleasure.

1106. Her embrace ever kindles new warm life in me. Verily her shoulders are packed with ambrosia.

1107. The embrace of my golden-coloured love reminds me of the joy of a householder who delights in fulfilling the laws of hospitality.

1108. Sweet indeed to both the lover and his beloved is that close embrace which allows not even a wisp of air to steal in between their arms.

1109. Separation, reconciliation and reunion are the pleasures vouchsafed to those stricken with love.

1110. The more I taste the charms of my beloved the more do I hunger for them. Verily what is already experienced pales into insignificance before the promise of the future.

CHAPTER 112—NALAM PUNAINDURAITTAL

1111. Nannīrai vāḻi: aniccamē! ninninum
mennīraḷ yāmvīḻ bavaḷ.

1112. malarkāṇin maiyātti neñje! Ivaḷkaṇ
palarkāṇum pūokkum eṉṟu.

1113. Muṟimēṉi muttam muṟuval veṟināṟṟam
vēluṇkaṇ vēyttōḷ avaṭku.

1114. Kāṇin kuvaḷai kaviḻndu nilaṉnokkum
māṇ iḻai kaṇ ovvēm eṉṟu.

1115. Aniccappūk kālkaḷaiyāḷ peytāḷ nus'uppiṟku
nalla paṭāa paṟai.

1116. Madiyum madandai mukaṉum aṟiyā
padiyil kalangiya mīṉ.

1117. Aṟuvāi niṟainda avirmadikkup pōla
maṟu uṇḍō mādar mukattu.

1118. Mādar mukampōl oḷiviḍa vallaiyēl
kādalai: vāḻi madi.

1119. Malaranna kaṇṇāḷ mukam otti āyin
palarkāṇat tōnṟal madi.

1120. Aniccamum annattin tūviyum mādar
aḍikku neruñjip paḻam.

CHAPTER 112—ON HIS LADY

1111. O **aniccam** flower, the best and softest of all flowers, may you be blest; but do not forget that my lady is yet more tender.

1112. O Mind, when you behold flowers you think that your beloved's eyes are like these and pine away.

1113. Her body is of rich gold, her teeth pearls. She is fragrant, her eyes dart forth glances like a lance, her shoulders gently curve as the bamboo. O! what a varied charm my beloved has!

1114. The **kundalai** flower hangs down in shame before the eyes of my tastefully adorned lady-love.

1115. She decks herself with **aniccam** flowers without removing the stalks. It is the death-knell of her slender waist.

1116. Even the stars of heaven veer their usual courses mistaking my lady's face for their queen moon.

1117. Is there a dark spot on the face of my lady-love as on the shining moon which waxes and wanes?

1118. Blest indeed are you, Moon! If you will be resplendent without a spot even as the face of my lady, I shall love you with all my heart.

1119. Moon, if you wish to equal the face of my lady then hide yourself from this world.

1120. The soft **aniccam** flower and the down of the swan are but thistles before the soft feet of my lady.

CHAPTER 113—KĀDAṞ S'IRAPPURAITTAL

1121. Pāloḍu tēṉkalan taṟṟē paṉimoḻi
vāl eyiṟu ūṟiya nīr.

1122. Uḍamboḍu uyiriḍai eṉṉamaṟ ṟaṉṉa
maḍandaiyoḍu emmiḍai naṭpu.

1123. Karumaṇiyil pāvāi ! ni podāi: yām vīḻum
tirunudaṟkku illai iḍam.

1124. Vāḻdal uyirkkaṉṉaḷ āyiḻai : s'ādal
adaṟkaṉṉaḷ nīngum iḍattu.

1125. Uḷḷuvaṉ maṉyaṉ maṟappiṉ maṟappaṟiyēṉ
oḷḷamark kaṇṇāḷ guṇam.

1126. Kaṇ uḷḷil pōkār: imaippiṉ paruvarār:
nuṇṇiyar em kādalavar.

1127. Kaṇullār kāda lavarāk kaṇṇum
eḻutēm karappākku aṟindu.

1128. Neñjattār kāda lavarāka veiduṇḍal
añjutum vēpākku aṟindu.

1129. Imaippiṉ karappāk kaṟival : aṉaittiṟkē
ēdilar eṉṉum ivvūr.

1130. Uvanduṟaivar uḷḷattuḷ eṉṟum ; ikanduṟaivar
ēdilar : eṉṉum ivvūr.

CHAPTER 113—ON THE AFFIRMATION OF LOVE

1121. The kiss of the tender lips of my modest maid is like the taste of honey with milk.

1122. The love that has sprung up between me and my beloved is constant, even as body and soul are inseparable.

1123. O Image in the pupil of my eye, begone! How can my fair-browed lady sit enthroned, unless you give place to her?

1124. Embracing the arms of my choicely adorned lady I feel all the thrill and joy of life, but the moment I separate, I feel the wretchedness of death.

1125. I cannot forget the noble quality of my love of the sparkling eyes.

1126. My lover will never vanish from my eyes; nor will he be disturbed if I close them. He is so ethereal as to be invisible.

1127. I fear to paint my eyes, lest it should hide the vision of my lord dwelling within.

1128. With my lover in my heart I do not eat anything hot lest it should harm the delicate one.

1129. My eyes wink not lest they should lose the vision of my lord within; not knowing this people blame him for my sleeplessness.

1130. Delightfully my lover makes my heart for ever his abode; but villainous people say he is cruel and dwells apart.

CHAPTER 114—NĀṆUTTUṚAVURAITTAL

1131. Kāmam uḷandu varundiṉārkku yēmam
maḍalalladu illai vali.

1132. Nōṉa uḍambum uyirum maḍaleṛum
nāṇiṉai nīkki niṛuttu.

1133. Nāṇoḍu nallāṇmai paṇḍuḍaiyēṉ : iṉṛuḍaiyēṉ
kāmuṛṛār ēṛum maḍal.

1134. Kāmak kaḍumpuṉal uykkumē nāṇoḍu
nallāṇmai eṉṉum puṇai.

1135. Toḍalaik kuṛuṁdoṭi tantāḷ maḍaloḍu
mālai uḷakkum tuyar.

1136. Maḍalūrdal yāmattum uḷḷuvēṉ : maṉṛa
paḍal ollā pēdaikkeṉ kaṇ.

1137. Kaḍalaṉṉa kāmam uḷandum maḍaleṛāp
peṇṇil perundakka til.

1138. Niṛaiariyar maṉṉaḷiyar eṉṉādu kāmam
maṛai iṛandu maṉṛu paḍum.

1139. Aṛikilār ellārum eṉṛēṉ kāmam
maṛukil maṛukum maruṇḍu.

1140. Yām kaṇṇil kāṇa naguba aṛivillār
yāmpaṭṭa tāmpaṭā vāru.

CHAPTER 114—SPEAKING OUT UNABASHED

1131. Men anguished by unrequited love find no stronger solace than mounting the **madal**.

1132. My body and soul, unequal to the pangs of love, seek to mount the **madal**; bashfulness and reserve are swept away.

1133. Reserve and dignified manliness once I had; but today I possess the **madal** which the helpless love-sick resort to.

1134. The giant force of the floods of love has carried away the raft of my manliness.

1135. The lady of little bracelets strung like garlands has taught me the love-sick pangs of evening and the **madal** horse. Never before have I known them.

1136. Thinking of this maid, my eyelids never close in slumber; even in dead of night my thoughts run on the suicidal **madal**.

1137. Woman tossed about in a sea of the anguish of love think not of mounting the **madal**—there is nothing greater than this.

1138. Oh my beloved! Wanton is my love which has no sympathy for my modesty or my helplessness; How it compels me to unpack my hidden secret and drag it out to the open!

1139. 'Nobody knows my secret' I said to myself; but my angry love rages in the market-place to my utter disgrace.

1140. Foolish people laugh at me before my very eyes; verily they have not experienced agony of love.

CHAPTER 115—ALARAṞIVUṞUTTAL

1141. Alar eḷa āruyir niṛkum : ataṉaip
palar aṛiyār baggiyattāl.

1142. Malar aṇṇa kaṇṇāḷ arumai aṛiyādu
alar emakku indadiv vūr.

1143. Uṛāadō ūraṛinda kauvai? ataṉaip
peṛādu peṛṛaṉṉa nīrttu.

1144. Kavvaiyāl kavvidu kāmam : adu iṉṛēl
tavveṉṉum taṉmai iḻandu.

1145. Kaḷittoṛum kaḷḷuṇḍal vēṭṭaṛṛāl : kāmam
veḷippaḍun tōrum iṉidu.

1146. Kaṇḍatu maṉṉum orunāḷ : alarmaṉṉum
tingaḷaip pāmpukoṇ daṛṛu.

1147. Ūravar kauvai eruvāka aṉṉaiśol
nīrāka nīḷum in nōy.

1148. Neyyāl erinuduppēm eṉṛaṛṛāl kauvaiyāl
kāmam nuduppēm eṉal.

1149. Alarnāṇa olvadō añjalōm peṉṛār
palaṛnāṇa nīttak kaḍai.

1150. Tām vēṇḍiṉ nalkuvar kādalár : yām vēṇḍum
kauvai eḍukkumiv vūr.

END OF KALAVIYAL

CHAPTER 115—RUMOURS OF SECRET LOVE

1141. The many scandals about our lòve do indeed give me fresh hope and sustain my wretched life. Luckily for me the village folk do not know what their scandals have done.

1142. Blind to the esteem of my lady of flower-like eyes, the village folk have linked her name with mine.

1143. Is not the rumour of this village sweet to me? For it makes me feel that I have attained the bliss of love even without my lover at my side.

1144. The rumours set afloat have heightened my love; but for these, it might lose its sweetness and wither away.

1145. Each cup adds to the gaiety of a revelling drunkard. Even so each rumour of our love adds to my delight.

1146. Only once have I seen him; but oh! rumours of our secret love have spread all over the vast world, even as the news of the serpent devouring the moon at an eclipse.

1147. How this plant of sickness grows on! The gossip of the village manures it and the frown of my mother waters it.

1148. With the scandals of the village one can never stifle love; it is like smothering fire with ghee.

1149. When my lover who swore not to leave me alone has abandoned me to the mockery of the many, why need I fear these tittle-tattle?

1150. This village rumour is useful; it has coupled you and your lover; the moment he desires, the lover can thus help us.

END OF THE SECRET UNION

II. KAṞPIYAL

CHAPTER 116—PIRIVĀṞṞĀMAI

1151. S'ellāmai uṇḍēl eṉakkurai; maṟṟu niṉ
valvaravu vāḻvārk kurai.

1152. Iṉkaṇ uḍaittavar pārval: pirivañcam
puṉkaṇ uḍaittāl puṇarvu.

1153. aridarō tēṟṟam arivuḍaiyār kaṇṇum
pirivōr iḍattuṇmai yāṉ.

1154. Aḷittañcal eṉṟavar nīppiṉ teḷittas'ol
teṟiyārkku uṇḍō tavaṟu.

1155. Ōmbiṉ amaindār pirivōmbal! maṟṟavar
nīngiṉ aridāl puṇarvu.

1156. Pirivuraikkum vaṉkaṇṇar āyin aridavar
Nalkuvar eṉṉum nas'ai.

1157. Tuṟaivaṉ tuṟandamai tūṟṟākol muṉkai
iṟai iṟavā niṉṟa vaḷai.

1158. Iṉṉādu iṉaṉ ilūr vāḻdal: adaṉiṉum
iṉṉādu iṉiyārp pirivu.

1159. Toḍins'uḍiṉ allatu kāmanōy pōla
viḍins'uḍal āṟṟumō tī.

1160. Aridāṟṟi allal nōy nīkkip pirivāṟṟip
piṉ irundu vāḻvār palar.

SECTION II—WEDDED LOVE

CHAPTER 116—THE PANGS OF SEPARATION

1151. If you are not to go away, tell me so that I may sustain my lingering life. If you are to go return soon.

1152. In the days of courtship what pleasure lay in each glance of his! Now after our union, the prospect of his separation brings gloom even in moments of happiness.

1153. Hard it is for me to rest assured; the lover who knows full well my miseries in separation still may part from me, making promises of quick return.

1154. How can there be blame on one who has put implicit trust in the comforting words of him who promised to shelter me for ever?

1155. Stop my lord from leaving me; only then can you save my life. Else it will flee at his parting and never again shall we meet.

1156. If he is cruel enough to speak of leaving me, I am lost; false it is to entertain any hope of his mercy.

1157. Will not the bracelets slipping loose from my wrist, tell the tale of the separation of my husband?

1158. Painful it is to live removed from familiar friends in a far-off village; but far more painful is the parting of the dearest one.

1159. Fire can scorch only when touched, but can it, like love, scorch persons away from it?

1160. Many ladies have gracefully borne news of separation, steered clear of sorrow, endured the parting of the loved one and still survived!

CHAPTER 117—PAḌARMELINDIRANGAL

1161. Maṟaippēṉmaṉ yāṉ ihdō nōyai iṟaippavarkku
ūṟṟunīr pōla mikum.

1162. Karattalum āṟṟēṉin nōyai nōy s'eydārkku
uraittalum nāṇut tarum.

1163. Kāmamum nāṇum uyirkāvāt tūngum eṉ
nōṉā uḍambiṉ akattu.

1164. Kāmak kaḍalmaṉṉum uṇḍē : adu nīndum
ēmap puṇaimaṉṉum il.

1165. Tuppiṉ evaṉāvar maṉkol tuyarvaravu
naṭpiṉul āṟṟu bavar.

1166. Iṉbam kaḍalmaṟṟuk kāmam ahdaḍunkāl
tuṉbam adaṉil peridu.

1167. Kāmak kaḍumpuṉal nīndik karaikāṇeṉ
yāmattum yāṉe uḷēṉ.

1168. maṉṉuyir ellām tuyiṟṟi aḷittirā
eṉalla tillai tuṇai.

1169. Koḍiyār koḍumaiyil tāmkoḍiya innāḷ
neḍiya kaḷiyum irā.

1170. Uḷḷampōṉṟu uḷvaḷic celkiṟpiṉ veḷḷanīr
nīndala maṉṉoeṉ kaṇ.

CHAPTER 117—THE CRY OF THE SEPARATED

1161. This my disease I seek to hide; but how endlessly it wells up like the waters of the spring.

1162. It lies not in my power to conceal the disease of my love. Nor am I able to speak of it unabashed to him who caused it.

1163. My frail body is harassed by love and my bashfulness bids me be quiet. My soul is torn between them.

1164. Verily the endless sea of love stretches before me; but I find not even a raft to cross the limitless expanse.

1165. Even to the loving one, he brings so much suffering; how much more pain will he cause to his enemy!

1166. Vast as the sea is the delight of wedded love; but vaster still are the sorrows of parting.

1167. Tossed in the troubled waters of love, I reach no shore; I am all alone in the still watches of the night.

1168. Beneficent night which has rocked all living creatures to sleep finds in me her lone sleepless companion.

1169. These nights, all too short in those sweet days, now lengthen their heavy hours, surpassing in cruelty even my lord.

1170. If only my eyes like my mind had the speedy power of fleeing to my lover, they need not now swim in a flood of tears.

CHAPTER 118—KAṆVIDUPPALIDAL

1171. Kaṇtām kaluḷvadu evaṉkolō taṇdānōy
tāmkāṭṭa yāmkaṇ ḍatu.

1172. Terinduṇarā nōkkiya uṇkaṇ parinduṇarāp
paidal uḷappadu evaṉ!

1173. Kadum eṉat tāmnōkkit tāmē kaluḷum
idunakat takka tuḍaittu.

1174. Peyal āṟṟā nīrulanda uṇkaṇ uyelāṟṟā
uyvil nōy eṉkaṇ niṟuttu.

1175. Paḍal āṟṟā paidal uḷakkum kaḍal āṟṟāk
kāma nōy s'eydaeṉ kaṇ.

1176. Ōo iṉide emakkinnōy s'eydakaṇ
tāam idaṉpaṭ ṭadu.

1177. Uḷanduḷandu uḷnīr aṟuka viḷaindiḷaindu
vēṇḍi avarkkaṇḍa kaṇ.

1178. Pēṇādu peṭṭār uḷarmaṉṉō! maṟṟavark
kāṇādu amaivila kaṇ.

1179. Vārākkāl tuñjā: variṉtuñjā: āyiḍai
ārajñar uṟṟaṉa kaṇ.

1180. Maṟaipeṟal urārkku aridaṇṟāl empōl
aṟaipaṟāi kaṇṇār akattu.

CHAPTER 118—ON EYES THAT LANGUISH

1171. Did you not show him to me and push me into the incurable sickness of love? Then why do you weep now to see him, the cause of all your woe?

1172. Oh Eyes! Having thoughtlessly feasted upon the lover, how can you now grieve for your own folly?

1173. Those eyes once leapt to see the lover: now they weep by themselves. Is it not laughable?

1174. Plunging me into an inevitable and incurable disease, these eyes of mine pour out their tears and run dry.

1175. My eyes that caused a disease of love vaster than the sea itself, do not now close themselves in sleep; they languish in grief.

1176. The very eyes that have caused me all those woes languish in sorrow by themselves. This is indeed just!

1177. These eyes hungered, wept, and repeatedly sent their glances to him. May they grieve and dry up all their stock of tears!

1178. She says to her companion: 'Did you not say that he who loves with words gets the wearing. Unless I see him straight before me, my eyelids do not close in sleep.'

1179. When he is away, my eyes are restless. When he comes, they are sleepless. Lost between these extremities my eyes endure untold suffering.

1180. It is certainly not hard for the villagers to read my secret love. My tell-tale eyes proclaim it to the world.

CHAPTER 119—PACAPPUṞU PARUVARAL

1181. Nayaṇḍavarkku nalkāmai nērndēṉ : pas'andaeṉ
paṇpiyārk kuraikkō piṟa.

1182. Avar dandār eṉṉum takaiyāl ivardandeṉ
mēṉimēḷ ūrum pacappu.

1183. S'āyalum nāṉum avarkoṇḍār kaimmāṟā
nōyum pas'alaiyum tandu.

1184. Uḷḷuvaṉ maṉyāṉ : uraippadu avartiṟamāl
kaḷḷam piṟavō pacappu.

1185. Uvakkāṉem kādalar s'elvār ivakkāṉeṉ
meṉi pacappūr vadu.

1186. Viḷakkaṟṟam pārkkum iruḷepōl koṇkaṉ
muyakkaṟṟam pārkkum pacappu.

1187. Pullik kiḍandēṉ puḍaipeyarndēṉ; avvaḷavil
aḷḷikkoḷ vaṟṟē pacappu.

1188. Pacandāḷ ivaḷ eṉbadu allāl ivaḷait
tuṟandār avareṉbār il.

1189. Pacakkamaṉ paṭṭāngeṉ mēṉi nayappittār
naṉṉilaiyar āva reṉiṉ.

1190. Pacappeṉap pērperudal naṉṟē nayappittār
nalkāmai tūṟṟār eṉiṉ.

CHAPTER 119—GRIEVING OVER LOVE'S PALLOR

1181. I did not assent to my lover's parting. To whom can I now complain of the pallor of my body, stricken with separation?

1182. The pallor spread over my body, exulting in the fact that he gave its birth.

1183. For my beauty and my bashfulness which he took away with him, my lover rewarded me with anguish and pallor.

1184. I think only of him and I open my lips only to sing his praises. Yet this pallor has come over me—O what cunning is this!

1185. Lo! Yonder is my lover gone. And here is the pallid hue spreading over my frame.

1186. Pallor awaits me the moment I am away from my lord's embrace, even as darkness lies in wait for the light to fade.

1187. I lay locked up in my lover's embrace; I moved away so little from him; when lo! pallor sprang up as it were to devour me.

1188. People say that I have gone sickly pale; never do they blame him that has abandoned me.

1189. If only he would keep his promise to return, my frame would gladly endure all the pallor of love.

1190. Good it is for me to be known as pallor incarnate if only people do not call my lover merciless.

CHAPTER 120—TAṈIPPAḌAR MIKUTI

1191. Tāmvīḻvār tamvīḻap peṟṟavar peṟṟārē
kāmattuk kāḻil kaṉi.

1192. Vāḻvārkku vāṉam payandaṟṟāl vīḻvārkku
vīḻvār aḷikkum aḷi.

1193. Vīḻunar vīḻap paḍuvārkku amaiyumē
vāḻunam eṉṉum s'erukku.

1194. Vīḻap paḍuvār keḻii ilar tāmvīḻvār
vīḻap paḍāar eṉiṉ.

1195. Nāmkādal koṇḍār namakkevaṉ s'eypavō
tāmkādal koḷḷāk kaḍai.

1196. Orutalaiyāṉ iṉṉādu kāmam : kāp pōla
irutalai yāṉum iṉidu.

1197. Paruvaralum paidalum kāṇāṉkol kāmaṉ
oruvarkaṇ niṉṟoḻuku vāṉ ?

1198. Vīḻvāriṉ iṉs'ol perādu ulakattu
vāḻvāriṉ vaṉkaṇār il.

1199. Nas'ai iyār nalkār eṉiṉum avarmāṭṭu
is'aiyum iṉiya s'evikku.

1200. Uṟāarkku uṟunōy uraippāy kaḍalaic
ceṟāa ai : vāḻiya neñcu.

CHAPTER 120—FEELING ALL ALONE

1191. Only those women taste all the juice of the seedless fruit of love, whose love is returned by their lovers.

1192. Welcome as the rain to the tillers of the earth is the grace of the lover to his loved one.

1193. Justly may those women feel proud of their life who are endowed with lovers who requite their love in all its fullness.

1194. Those whose love is not returned by their sweet ones are unlucky beyond measure. Of what avail to them is the esteem of others ?

1195. When he does not return my love, what favour can I expect of him ?

1196. Bitter is unrequited love; sweet it is if returned in equal measure like the well-poised even scales.

1197. Cannot the god of love, who pays his attention to me alone, behold all my anguish and sorrow ?

1198. Breathes there a more cruel soul on this earth than the one who lives on without the encouraging words of the loved one ?

1199. Though the loved one favours me not, delightful indeed is stray news of him that reaches my ears.

1200. Oh my heart! try to tell gnawing cares to your unresponsive lover; you may as well strive to dry up the surging sea.

CHAPTER 121—NINAINDAVAR PULAMBAL

1201. Uḷḷinum tīrāp perumakiḻ s'eydalāl
kaḷḷinum kāmam iṉiḍu.

1202. Eṉaittoṉṟu iṉitēkāṇ kāmam ; tām vīḻvār
niṉaippa varuvatoṉṟu il.

1203. Niṉaippavar pōṉṟu niṉaiyār kol ; tummal
s'iṉaippadu pōṉṟu keḍum.

1204. Yāmum uḷēmkol avar neñcattu emneñcattu
ōo uḷarē avar.

1205. Tamneñcattu emmaik kaḍikoṇḍār nāṇārkol
emneñcattu ōvā varal.

1206. Maṟṟuyāṉ eṉuḷēṉ maṉṉō ? avaroḍuyāṉ
uṟṟanāḷ uḷḷa uḷēṉ.

1207. Maṟappiṉ evaṉ āvaṉ maṉkol ? maṟappṟiyēṉ
uḷḷiṉum uḷḷam s'uḍum.

1208. Eṉaittu niṉaippiṉum kāyār : aṉaittaṉṟō
kādalar s'eyyum s'iṟappu.

1209. Viḷiyum eṉ iṉuyir vēṟallam eṉbār
aḷiiṉmai āṟṟa niṉaindu.

1210. Viḍādu s'eṉṟāraik kaṇṇiṉāl kāṇap
paḍāadi : vāḷi : mati.

CHAPTER 121—RECOLLECTING THE PLEASURES OF LOVE

1201. Love is far sweeter than wine; for unlike wine the very thought of love intoxicates me.

1202. Love is sweet in all respects; the thought of the dear one even in separation tastes sweet.

1203. She says to her companion: "A sneeze comes upon me but goes away all of a sudden; perhaps a thought of me occurs to him and then he forgets it."

1204. He is ever present in my thoughts. Am I or am I not ever present in his thoughts?

1205. He keeps me away from his heart; does he not feel ashamed of constantly stealing into my heart?

1206. Only the recollection of those ecstatic days with him makes me live. What else can sustain me?

1207. Never have I forgotten the golden days with my beloved; his separation now burns into my heart; certain is death if ever the memory of him forsakes my luckless heart.

1208. However much I may think of him, he is never angry with me. Inimitable is my lover's grace.

1209. As I think and think of the cruelty of my love who swore that our lives were inseparable, my soul ebbs away.

1210. She says to the moon: "O blessed moon! Ceaselessly pour your rays till I am able to see with my eyes the loved one who has forsaken me but yet dwells for ever in my heart."

CHAPTER 122—KAṈAVUNILAI URAITTAL

1211. Kādalar tūtoḍu vanda kaṉaviṉukku
yādus'ey vēṉkoḷ virundu.

1212. Kayal uṇkaṇ yāṉirappat tuññjiṉ kalandārkku
uyal uṇmai s'āṟṟuvēṉ maṉ.

1213. Naṉaviṉāl nalkā tavaraik kaṉaviṉāl
kāṇḍaliṉ uṇḍeṉ uyir.

1214. Kaṉaviṉāṉ uṇḍāgum kāmam naṉaviṉāṉ
nalkārai nāḍit taraṟku.

1215. Naṉaviṉāṉ kaṇḍatūum āngē kaṉavundāṉ
kaṇḍa poḻutē iṉidu.

1216. Naṉaveṉa oṉṟillai yāyiṉ kaṉaviṉāl
kādalar nīngalar maṉ.

1217. Naṉaviṉāl nalkāk koḍiyār kaṉaviṉāṉ
eṉemmaip pīḻip padu.

1218. Tuññjumkāl tōḷmēlar āki viḻikkumkāl
neññcatta rāvar viraindu.

1219. Naṉaviṉāṉ nalkārai nōvar kaṉaviṉāl
kādalark kāṇā davar.

1220. Naṉaviṉāṉ namnīttār eṉbar kaṉaviṉāṉ
kāṇārkol ivvū ravar.

CHAPTER 122—DREAMS OF LOVE

1211. With what feast may I entertain the dream that has brought glad tidings of my lover ?

1212. If only my eyes would close in sleep at my request, how I would meet him in dreams !

1213. The merciless one favours me not in waking hours ; but in dreams I feast on him and thus manage to live.

1214. Why do I love dreams ? It is because they bring before me the one who in waking hours favours me not.

1215. Sweet is his presence in the waking hours ; sweet too is his appearance in a dream. What then do I miss in seeing him in my dreams ?

1216. If only there was no such thing as waking hours, my lover would never desert me in my dreams.

1217. Why does the cruel one plague me in my dreams when he shows no compassion on me in my waking state ?

1218. She says to her companion : "He embraces me in my dreams but the moment I awake he quickly vanishes into my heart."

1219. Only those women who do not see their lovers in dreams, blame them for their cruelty in waking hours.

1220. Folk say : "He has abandoned her in sooth." Verily they do not know how he visits me in my dreams.

CHAPTER 123—POḺUTU KAṆḌIRANGAL

1221. Mālaiyō allai; maṉantār uyiruṇṇum
vēlainī; vāḻi poḻutu.

1222. Puṉkaṇṇai; vāḻī; maruḷmālai emkēḷpōl
vaṉkaṇṇa tōniṉ tuṇai.

1223. Paṉi arumbip paidalkoḷ mālai tuṉi arumbit
tuṉbam vaḷara varum.

1224. Kādalar ilvaḻi mālai kolaikkaḷattu
ēdilar pōla varum.

1225. Kālaikkuc ceydanaṉ ṟeṉkol evaṉkolyāṉ
mālaikkuc ceyda pakai.

1226. Mālainōy ceydal maṇandār akalāta
kālai aṟindatu ilēṉ.

1227. Kālai arumbip pakalellām pōdāki
mālai malarumin nōy.

1228. Aḻalpōlum mālaikkut tūdāki āyaṉ
kuḻalpōlum kollum paḍai.

1229. Padimaruṇḍu paidal uḻakkum madimaruṇḍu
mālai paṭartarum pōḻtu.

1230. Poruḷmālai āḷarai uḷḷi maruḷmālai
māyumeṉ māyā uyir.

CHAPTER 123—SUNSET AND SORROW

1221. O blessed twilight! You are not the twilight of the joyous old times; you are the end of the world devouring the lives of the parted lovers.

1222. "Blest be thou, O twilight! You are pale and your eyes are lustreless. Is your sweet one as cruel as mine?"

1223. O Evening! In those joyous days with my beloved you approached me timidly with drops of dew on you and sadness written in your face. Your advance now brings with it only distaste and sorrow.

1224. My lover away, evening comes murderously like a hangman rushing to the place of slaughter.

1225. Morning, Evening, why should these alternately assuage and afflict me in this separation? What good have I done to morn and what harm to even?

1226. With my lover by my side, never for once, did I taste the bitterness that eventide can cause.

1227. This disease of love buds in the morning, grows and grows all day long and flowers into full bloom at eventide.

1228. The note of the shepherd's pipe, which sounded so pleasant in the happy days, has now become a message of the hot evening—verily a weapon forging my death.

1229. When senseless evening creeps painfully along, the whole village feels dizzy and is plunged in the anguish of separation.

1230. This life of mine which has survived this bitter separation is very near to death in this treacherous evening, as I think of my lord who values riches far above love.

CHAPTER 124—UṞUPPU NALAṈ AḶITAL

1231. S'iṟumai namakkoḷiyac cēṇceṉḍṟār uḷḷi
naṟumalar nāṇiṉa kaṇ.

1232. Nayandavar nalkāmai s'olluva pōlum
pacandu paṉivārum kaṇ.

1233. Taṉandamai s'āla aṟivippa pōlum
maṉandanāḷ vīṅgiya tōḷ.

1234. Paṇainīṅgip paindoṭi s'ōrum tuṇainīṅgit
tolkaviṉ vāḍiya tōḷ.

1235. Koḍiyār koḍumai uraikkum toḍiyoḍu
tolkaviṉ vāḍiya tōḷ.

1236. Toḍiyoḍu tōḷnekiḷa nōval avaraik
koḍiyar eṉakkūṟal nondu.

1237. Pāḍu peṟutiyō neñcē! koḍiyārkku eṉ
vāḍutōḷ pūs'al uraittu.

1238. Muyangiya kaikaḷai ūkkap pacandatu
paintoḍip pēdai nudal.

1239. Muyakkiḍait taṇvaḷi pōlap pacappuṟṟa
pēdai perumaḷaik kaṇ.

1240. Kaṇṇiṉ pacappō paruvaral eytiṉṟē
oḷnudal seydatu kaṇḍu.

CHAPTER 124—WASTING AWAY

1231. Companion to lady-love: "Stop this weeping and wailing. The thought of the one gone far away has made your eyes pale and lustreless."

1232. "Your pallid eyes streaming with tears proclaim the callousness of your lord."

1233. "Your shoulders that swelled with joy on the day of your marriage are thin today; they proclaim how your lord has cruelly forsaken you."

1234. "Since your separation from your lord your shoulders have lost their innate grace; worse still they have become lanky; and the bangles too slip on your slender arms."

1235. My bracelets slip; the charm of my shoulders withers away. It proclaims the cruelty of the heartless one.

1236. With loose bangles and leaner shoulders, I still feel pained to hear him called cruel; I cannot bear any affront to my lord's fair name.

1237. "O my heart, do you desire to cover yourself with glory? Then go to the cruel one and tell him the wasting away of my shoulders and these rumours of cruelty abroad."

1238. He soliloquising: "once when I gently loosened my hands from an ecstatic embrace, the forehead of my love suddenly turned pale. I wonder how she bears my separation in these long days."

1239. "The still eyes of my love dark as the rain-bearing cloud turned sickly pale the moment a gust of wind crept in between our locked arms; how does she bear the estranging seas and mountains hurled in between us now?"

1240. "Her eyes turned lustreless at the release of my arms from their close embrace; was it in sympathy with the fading brightness of her forehead?"

CHAPTER 125—NEÑCOḌU KIḶATTAL

1241. Niṉaittoṉṟu s'ollāyō neñcē! eṉaittoṉṟum
evvamnōy tīrkkum maṟundu.

1242. Kādal avarilar ākanī nōvatu
pēdaimai vāḷi; eṉ neñcu!

1243. Irunduḷḷi eṉbaridal: neñcē! parinduḷḷal
paidalnōy ceydārkaṇ il.

1244. Kaṇṇum koḷaccēṟi neñcē! ivai eṉṉait
tiṉṉum avarkkāṇal uṟṟu.

1245. Ceṟṟār eṉakkai viḍaluṇḍō neñcēyām!
uṟṟāl uṟā davar.

1246. Kalanduṇarndum kādalark kaṇḍāl pulanduṇarāy
poykkāyvu kāyti: eṉ neñcu.

1247. Kāmam viḍuoṉṟō nāṇviḍu: eṉ neñcē!
yāṉō poṟēniv viraṇḍu.

1248. Parindavar nalkāreṉ ṟēngip pirindavar
piṉs'elvāy pēdai eṉ neñcu.

1249. Uḷḷattār kāda lavarāka uḷḷinī
yāruḷaic cēṟieṉ neñcu.

1250. Tuṉṉāt tuṟandārai neñcat tuḍaiyēmā
iṉṉum iḷattum kaviṉ.

CHAPTER 125—SOLILOQUY OF THE LADY-LOVE

1241. O heart! can you not cast about and find a remedy for my lovesickness which causes me such sorrow?

1242. 'Blessed may you be O heart! how foolish of you to bemoan separation when he has no love for you!

1243. 'O heart! Why stay in vain here and feel wretched? There is no sympathy in the heart of him who has caused you this wasting disease.

1244. 'O my heart! if you go to him, take my eyes also with you. They eat into my being in their craving to see him.'

1245. 'O heart! can I really forsake him as cruel though he has used me cruelly when I clung to him.'

1246. O my heart! could you ever bear even a mock quarrel with your lover to sweeten his company? Then why call him cruel now for your own fault?

1247. My good heart! cast off one of the two—love or bashfulness. I cannot bear the insupportable weight of them both.

1248. 'You go seeking with a hopeless aching heart after the far-off lover, because he has not understood and favoured you with his mercy. O foolish heart!'

1249. 'O my heart, is it you keep your lover within you? Then whom do you search in your thoughts? Why search for him outside? Whom do you hope to reach?'

1250. The more I have him in my heart who has left me never to come back, the more my beauty wastes away.

CHAPTER 126—NIṚAI AḺITAL

1251. Kāmak kaṇicci uḍaikkum niṛaiennum
nāṇuttāḷ vīḻttaḵkadavu.

1252. Kāmam enaoṇṛō kaṇinṛen neñcattai
yāmattum āḷum toḻil.

1253. Maṛaippēṉmaṉ kāmattai yāṉō : kuṛippiṉṛit
tummalpōl tōṉṛi viḍum.

1254. Niṛaiuḍaiyēṉ eṉbēṉmaṉ : yāṉōeṉ kāmam
maṛaiiṛandu maṉṛu paḍum.

1255. S'eṟṟārpiṉ s'ellāp perundakaimai kāmanōy
uṟṟār aṛivadoṉṛu aṉṛu.

1256. S'eṟṟavar piṉs'ēral vēṇḍi aḻittarō !
eṟṟeṉṉai uṟṟa tuyar.

1257. Nāṇeṉa oṉṛō aṛiyalam kāmattāl
pēṇiyār peṭba ceyiṉ.

1258. Paṉmāyak kaḷvaṉ paṇimoḻi yaṉṟō nam
peṇmai uḍaikkum paḍai.

1259. Pulappal eṉac ceṉṟēṉ : pulliṉēṉ neñcam
kalattal uṛuvadu kaṇḍu.

1260. Niṇamtīyil iṭṭaṉṉa neñciṉārk kuṇḍō
puṇarndūṭi niṟpēm eṉal.

CHAPTER 126—ON LOSS OF MODESTY

1251. The door of my maidenly grace and the bolt and bars of modesty are hewn by the weapon of restless love.

1252. Verily the thing called love has no grace; even at dead of night it rules my heart and keeps it awake when all the world is in slumber.

1253. I strive to hide this my passion. Yet it breaks out against my wish like a sudden sneeze.

1254. I pride myself on my modesty. But my passion breaks all barriers and brings me out into the open.

1255. Victims of passion can never understand the nobility of giving up the pursuit of unrequited love.

1256. How cruel is the malady which sends me after the heartless one! Mine is indeed a pitiable lot.

1257. When the loved one, after all his vagaries, took me into his loving embraces all my bashfulness fled away.

1258. The weapon that shatters our maidenly reserve is none other than the talk of the artful lover.

1259. With the fixed resolve of forsaking him I went, but my heart yielded to his embrace.

1260. People with hearts melting like fat at the touch of fire—how can they reject the offered love and stand aloof?

CHAPTER 127—AVARVAYIṈ VIDUMBAL

1261. Vāḷ aṛṛup puṛkeṉṛa kaṇṇum : avar s'eṉṛa
nāḷoṛṛit tēynda, viral.

1262. Ilankiḷāy ! iṉṛu maṛappiṉeṉ tōḷmēl
kalankaḻiyum kārikai nīttu.

1263. Uraṉnas'aii uḷḷam tuṇaiyākac ceṉṛār
varal nas'aii iṉṉum uḷēṉ.

1264. Kūḍiya kāmam pirindār varavuḷḷik
kōḍukoṇḍeṛum eṉ neñcu.

1265. Kāṇkamaṉ koṇkaṉaik kaṇṇārak kaṇḍapiṉ
nīngumeṉ meṉtōḷ pas'appu.

1266. Varukamaṉ koṇkaṉ orunāḷ parukuvaṉ
paidalnōy ellām keḍa.

1267. Pulappēṉkol pulluvēṉ kollō kalappēṉkol
kaṇaṉṉa kēḷir variṉ.

1268. Viṉaikalandu veṉṛīka vēndaṉ : maṉaikalandu
mālai ayarkam virundu.

1269. Orunāḷ eḻunāḷpōṛ s'ellum s'ēṇ s'eṉṛār
varunāḷvaittu ēngu pavarkku.

1270. Peṛiṉeṉṉām peṛṛakkāl eṉṉām uṛiṉeṉṉām
uḷḷam uḍaindukkak kāl,

CHAPTER 127—ON DISTRESS OF EACH TOWARDS THE OTHER

1261. Counting the days of his separation, my fingers have become wasted and worn out; my eyes have grown dim and faint.

1262. O! bright girl, if I forget my lord today, then my shoulders will become thin and my bangles loose.

1263. I continue to live in eager expectation of the return of my lover. He took with him as his friend his own brave heart.

1264. With the thought of my lover's return anxious for reunion, my heart goes on climbing higher and higher.

1265. After feasting my eyes with the sight of my husband, my soft shoulders will lose their pallor.

1266. Let my husband come here one day. Then my wasting disease will be completely cured.

1267. When my husband, dear to me as my eyes, returns, shall I be indifferent or complaining? Shall I not be one with him?

1268. May my lord be victorious in action and may I also go home to enjoy my evening repast with a guest.

1269. To one who awaits the day of arrival of her husband, one day appears as long as seven.

1270. If her heart has been broken, of what avail is it if I become available to her, reach her or even join her?

CHAPTER 128—KUṞIPPAṞIVUṞUTTAL

1271. Kă̆rappiṉum kai ikandu ollāniṉ uṇkaṇ
uraikkal uṟuvatoṉṟu uṇḍu.

1272. Kaṇṇiṟainda kārikaik kāmpērtōḷ pēdaikkup
peṇṇiraința nīrmai peritu.

1273. Maṇiyil tikaḷtaru nūlpōl maḍantai
aṇiyil tikaḷvadoṉṟu uṇḍu.

1274. Mukaimokkuḷ uḷḷatu nāṟṟampōl pēdai
nakaimokkuḷ uḷḷatoṉṟu uṇḍu.

1275. S'eritoḍi s'eytiṟanda kaḷḷam uṟutuyar
tīrkkum marundoṉṟu uḍaittu.

1276. Peritāṟṟip peṭpak kalattal aritāṟṟi
aṉbiṉmai s'ūḷvatu uḍaittu.

1277. Taṇṇam tuṟaivaṉ taṇantamai nammiṉum
muṉṉam uṇarnta vaḷai.

1278. Nerunaṟṟu ceṉṟār enkātalar: yāmum
eḻunāḷēm mēṉi pas'andu.

1279. Toḍinōkki meṉtōḷum nōkki aḍinōkki
ahdāṇḍu avaḷs'ey tatu.

1280. Peṇṇiṉāl peṇmai uḍaitteṉba kaṇṇiṉāl
kāmanōy s'olli iravu,

CHAPTER 128—ON SPEAKING ON THE SIGNS

1271. Though you hide it, your uncontrolled eyes reveal a secret to me.

1272. This girl of long eyes and bamboo shoulders has too much womanly modesty.

1273. Just like the thread concealed by the beads there is something lying beneath this damsel's beauty.

1274. Even as the fragrance that is locked up in the bud, there is something hidden in this damsel's smile.

1275. The tactful departure of my bangled lady serves as soothing balm for my excruciating pain.

1276. The pleasant union after the distress of separation still reminds one of the past indifference of the lover.

1277. My bangles betrayed even before I did my lover's separation from me.

1278. It was only yesterday that my lover went, but I have acquired seven days' pallor.

1279. She looks at her bangles; she looks at her beautiful shoulders and she looks down at her feet. This is her present occupation.

1280. The eyes seek the cure of passion. It is the modesty of a modest woman.

CHAPTER 129—PUṆARCCI VIDUMBAḶ

1281. Uḷḷak kaḷittalum kāṇamakiḻ talum
kaḷḷukkil: kāmattiṟku uṇḍu.

1282. Tiṉaittuṇaiyum ūḍāmai vēṇḍum paṉaittuṇaiyum
kāmam niṟaiya variṉ.

1283. Peṇātu peṭpavē s'eyyiṉum koṇkaṉaik
kāṇātu amaiyala kaṇ.

1284. Ūḍaṟkaṇ s'eṉṟēnmaṉ tōḻi adumaṟandu
kūḍaṟkaṇ s'eṉṟateṉ neñcu.

1285. Eḻutunkāl kōlkāṇāk kaṇṇēpōl koṇkaṉ
paḻikāṇēṉ kaṇḍa viḍattu.

1286. Kāṇunkāl kāṇēṉ tavaṟāya: kāṇākkāl
kāṇēṉ tavaṟal lavai.

1287. Uyttal aṟindu puṉalpāy pavarēpōl
poyttal aṟindeṉ pulandu.

1288. Iḷittakka iṉṉā s'eyiṉun kaḷittārkkuk
kaḷḷaṟṟē kaḷva ! niṉ mārpu.

1289. Malariṉun mellitu kāmam: s'ilaradaṉ
s'evvi talaippaḍu vār.

1290. kaṇṇil tuṉittē kalangiṉāḷ pulludal
eṉṉiṉum tāṉvidup puṟṟu.

CHAPTER 129—ON YEARNING AFTER UNION

1281. To become pleased with the thought and happy at the sight of the lover, these are the fruits not of wine but of love.

1282. If a woman's passion becomes excessive, she should avoid even slight misunderstanding.

1283. Though my husband acts regardless of me, yet my eyes cannot be satisfied without seeing him.

1284. O Friend! I went to quarrel with him; but forgetting it my heart sought for reconciliation.

1285. Just as our eyes do not see the pen when writing I could not see my lover's faults when I saw him.

1286. When I see my husband I cannot see his faults. In his absence I cannot see anything else.

1287. Of what avail is it to sift all the lies of one's husband! It is as ineffectual as a diver battling with an irresistible current.

1288. O cheat! your breast is coveted more and more even as liquor with all its harm is by the drunkard.

1289. More tender than a flower is love and few are they who enjoy it fully.

1290. With resentful eyes, my lady complained: but eager for reconciliation she forget her anger.

CHAPTER 130—NEÑCOḌU PULATTAL

1291. Avarneñcu avarkkādal kaṇḍum evaṉneñcē
nī emakku ākā tatu.

1292. Uṟā tavarkkaṇḍa kaṇṇum avaraic
ceṟāreṉac cēṟiyeṉ neñcu.

1293. Keṭṭārkku naṭṭāril eṉbatō neñcē nī
peṭṭāngu avarpiṉ s'elal.

1294. Iṉiaṉṉa niṉṉoḍu s'ūḻvāryār neñcē
tuṉis'eydu tuvvāikāṇ maṟṟu.

1295. Peṟāmai añcum peṟinpirivu añcum
aṟā iḍumbaitteṉ neñcu.

1296. Taṉiyē irundu niṉaittakkāl eṉṉait
tiṉiya irundadeṉ neñcu.

1297. Nāṇum maṟantēṉ avarmaṟak kallāeṉ
māṇā maḍaneñcil paṭṭu.

1298. Eḷḷiṉ iḷivāmeṉṟu eṇṇi avartiṟam
uḷḷum uyirkkādal neñcu.

1299. Tuṇbattiṟkku yārē tuṇaiyāvār tāmuḍaiya
neñcam tuṇaial vaḷi.

1300. Tañcam tamarallar ētilār tāmuḍaiya
neñcam tamaral vaḷi.

CHAPTER 130—ON SPEAKING WITH THE MIND

1291. O! My heart, though you know that my husband's heart thinks only of himself, how is it you think of him and not of me?

1292. O! My heart, knowing that he has no thought for you, still you run after him expecting no refusal.

1293. O! My heart, you go after him without my permission. Is it because none will befriend those in adversity?

1294. O! My heart, if you see him, you do not resent his faults. Who can consult you for advice?

1295. My mind can have only endless anxiety; for I fear both when he is with me and also without me.

1296. My heart eats me up when I think of him in my loneliness.

1297. With my foolish heart remembering him who has forgotten me, I have forgotten even my sense of shame.

1298. My heart that loves life and views it ignoble to blame and to deny access to him, ever thinks of his success.

1299. Who will be a friend in misery but one's own heart?

1300. If one's own heart turns against one, how can one expect anything but hostility from others?

CHAPTER 131—PULAVI

1301. Pullā tirāap pulattai : avaruṟum
allalnōy kāṇkam s'iritu.

1302. Uppamain taṟṟāl pulavi : adus'iṟitu
mikkaṟṟāl nīḷa viḍal.

1303. Alandārai allalnōy s'eydaṟṟāl tammaip
pulandāraip pullā viḍal.

1304. Ūḍi yavarai uṇarāmai vāḍiya
vaḷḷi mudalarin daṟṟu.

1305. Nalattakai nallavark kēr pulattakai
pūaṉṉa kaṇṇār akattu.

1306. Tuṉiyum pulaviyum il āyiṉ kāmam
kaṉiyum karukkāyum aṟṟu.

1307. Ūḍaliṉ uṇḍāngōr tuṉbam puṇarvatu
nīḍuvadu aṉṟukol eṉṟu.

1308. Nōdal evaṉmaṟṟu nondāreṉṟu ahtaṟiyum
kādalar illā vaḷi.

1309. Nīrum niḻalatu iṉitē : pulaviyum
vīḻunar kaṇṇē iṉitu.

1310. Ūḍal uṇanga viḍuvārōḍu eṉneñcam
kūḍuvēm eṉbadu avā..

CHAPTER 131—ON LOVERS' MISUNDERSTANDING

1301. Let us see a little his distress in passion, by showing reserve.

1302. Reserve like a pinch of salt adds to enjoyment. If excessive, it spoils the taste.

1303. If men do not pacify women who feign coolness, it is like causing more pain to those who already suffer.

1304. Not to pacify the lady who feigns coolness is to cut the withering creeper away at the root.

1305. The beauty of a loyal lover is only enhanced by the reserve of his flower-eyed lady.

1306. If indignation and gentle resentment are absent, love will be like fruit over-ripe or unripe.

1307. There is anxiety and pain in lovers' uncertain quarrels.

1308. If a lover were to be blind to the suffering of the lady-love, then the suffering would be in vain.

1309. Just as water in the shade is sweet, so lovers' quarrels become sweet only to people deep-rooted in love.

1310. My heart longs for reunion with him who cares not for my sufferings in the quarrel.

CHAPTER 132—PULAVI NUṆUKKAM

1311. Peṇ iyalār ellārum kaṇṇil podu uṇpar
naṇṇēṉ parattaṉiṉ mārpu.

1312. Ūḍi irundēmāt tumminār yāmtammai
nīḍuvāḻ keṉbāk kaṛindu.

1313. Kōṭṭuppūc cūḍiṉum kāyum oruttiyaik
kāṭṭiya s'ūḍiṉīr eṉṟu.

1314. Yāriṉum kādalam eṉṟēṉā ūḍināḷ
yāriṉum yāṟiṉum eṉṟu.

1315. Immaip piṟappil piriyalam eṉṟēṉāk
kaṇṇiṟai nīrkoṇ ḍaṉaḷ.

1316. Uḷḷiṉēṉ eṉṟēṉ : maṟṟeṉ maṟandīr eṉṟeṉṉaip
pullāḷ pulattak kaṉaḷ.

1317. Vaḻuttiṉāḷ tummiṉēṉ āka : aḻittaḻutāḷ
yāruḷḷit tummiṉīr eṉṟu.

1318. Tummuc ceṟuppa aḻudāḷ numaruḷḷal
emmai maṟaittirō eṉṟu.

1319. Taṉṉai uṇarttiṉum kāyum piṟarkkunīr
innīrar ākutir eṉṟu.

1320. Niṉaittirundu nōkkiṉum kāyum aṉaittunīr
yāruḷḷi nōkkiṉīr eṉṟu.

CHAPTER 132—ON SUBTLETY OF LOVERS' MISUNDERSTANDING

1311. You yielded yourself to all sorts of women to look at you with their eyes. Therefore I shall not approach your breast.

1312. When I sat away from him, he sneezed knowing that I would bless him, saying " May you live long."

1313. Even if I put on a garland of hill-flowers, my sweetheart will say " You wore this to please some mistress of yours."

1314. When I said my beloved was greater than anybody else, she grew angry and repeatedly asked me " Greater than whom ? "

1315. When I said "We shall not separate in this life ", her eyes were full of tears meaning that I would separate from her in the next life.

1316. When I said 'I thought of you', she replied " So you forgot me before " and felt displeased.

1317. When I sneezed she blessed me ; but she wept and asked me which maiden thought of me when I sneezed.

1318. When I controlled sneezing, she shed fretful tears, and asked whether I tried to conceal the fact that others think of me.

1319. She will quarrel with me even if I fully satisfy her, saying " You will behave thus to every woman."

1320. If I look at her silently and appreciate her beauty, she will ask me querulously, " whom you are thinking of ? "

CHAPTER 133—ŪḌALUVAKAI

1321. Illai tavaṛavarkku āyiṉum ūḍutal
vallatavar aḷikkum āṛu.

1322. Ūḍalil tōṉṛum s'iṛutuṉi nalaḷi
vāḍiṉum pāḍu peṛum.

1323. Pulattalil puttēḷnāḍu uṇḍō nilattoḍu
nīriyain daṉṉār akattu.

1324. Pulli viḍāap pulaviyuḷ tōṉṛumeṉ
uḷḷam uḍaikkum paḍai.

1325. Tavaṛilar āyiṉum tāmvīḻvār meṉṛōḷ
akaṛaliṉ āngoṉ ṛuṭaittu.

1326. Uṇaliṉum uṇḍa taṛal iṉitu : kāmam
puṇardaliṉ ūḍal iṉitu.

1327. Ūḍalil tōṛṛavar veṉṛār : adumaṉṉum
kūḍalil kāṇap paḍum.

1328. Ūḍip perukuvam kollō nudalveyarppak
kūdalil tōṉṛiya uppu.

1329. Ūḍuka maṉṉō oḷi iḷai : yāmirappa
nīḍuka maṉṉō irā.

1330. Ūḍutal kāmattiṛku iṉbam : ataṛku iṉbam
kūḍi muyangap peṛiṉ.

END OF KĀMATTUPPĀL

CHAPTER 133—ON THE PLEASURES OF LOVERS' MISUNDERSTANDING

1321. Though he is guiltless, false accusations make him more attached.

1322. The little resentment resulting from lover's quarrels yields delight in the end, though it may for the moment seem to cause pain.

1323. Is there any other heaven than the quarrel between lovers whose minds are united even as earth and water?

1324. The weapon that breaks my obstinate heart lies in the quarrel itself.

1325. Though guiltless being denied, there is a pleasure in the embrace of the soft beautiful shoulders of the sweetheart.

1326. Sweeter than eating is the pause in the process. Likewise misunderstanding by lovers affords more joy than union itself.

1327. In a lovers' quarrel, the vanquished becomes the victor; this is revealed when they reunite.

1328. Am I likely to gain, after a friendly quarrel, the delight now experienced in the union with her moistened forehead?

1329. May the jewelled lady-love go on quarrelling; may also the night be long enough to conciliate her!

1330. The delight of love is the lovers' quarrel; greater delight is the loving reunion.

END OF KĀMATTUPPĀL